Proceeds from this book will be donated by Chinook Centre to local literacy groups, through the Canwest Raise-a-Reader program.

Copyright © 2009 Chinook Centre

All rights reserved. No part of this book may be reproduced, sorted in a retrieval system or transmitted, in any form or by any means, without the prior written consent of Chinook Centre.

Chinook Centre; 6455 Macleod Trail S.W.; Calgary, Alberta; Canada; T2H 0K8; (403) 259-2022
chiinfo@cadillacfairview.com; www.chinookcentre.com

Library and Archives Canada Cataloguing in Publication

Zurowski, Monica

Chinook Centre: a city within a city : fifty years of people, progress,

vision and values / by Monica Zurowski.

ISBN 978-0-9813383-0-9

1. Chinook Centre--History. 2. Calgary (Alta.)--History. I. Chinook

Centre II. Title.

HF5430.6.C3Z87 2009   381'.1109712338   C2009-905601-1

Thank you to the community of Calgary and all its residents who have supported Chinook Centre over the decades. Also, thanks are extended to the employees, managers and owners who have helped grow and develop the shopping centre.

Special thanks to the Calgary Herald for use of its archives, articles and photos, to the Glenbow Archives and to the Calgary Public Library.

Chinook Centre: A City Within a City
Fifty Years of People, Progress, Vision & Values

By Monica Zurowski

Research and additional writing by Karen Crosby and Norma Marr

Design by Janet Matiisen and Kathryn Molcak

Photography by Grant Black

Editing by Brent Morrison

Pre-press photo work by Andrew Gilluley

Printed and bound in Canada by Friesens
First edition

CHINOOK CENTRE
A CITY WITHIN A
CITY

Fifty Years of People, Progress,
Vision & Values

CONTENTS

CHINOOK CENTRE

MAY 12, 1949
Chinook Drive-In Theatre opens.

SEPT. 20, 1957
Woodward's announces it will build a new store in Calgary, in a proposed massive shopping centre in the city's southwest.

MAY 2, 1958
The location of the proposed shopping centre changes from Elbow Drive and 82nd Avenue S.W. to the site of the Chinook Drive-In on Macleod Trail.

SEPTEMBER 1958
The Chinook Drive-In closes.

SEPT. 19, 1958
Sod-turning ceremony is held for the Chinook Shopping Centre.

CALGARY & AREA

1947
Calgary's population hits 100,000.

FEB. 13, 1947
The Leduc No. 1 well blows, cementing Alberta's reputation as an energy powerhouse.

1950
A three-bedroom Calgary home costs $13,500; car prices average $1,625; and a gallon of gas is 17 cents.

DEC. 28, 1951
Business activity in Calgary grows by 21 per cent in just one year.

OCT. 3, 1954
Television service begins in the city.

DEC. 6, 1954
One-way traffic is implemented on some Calgary streets.

JULY 19, 1955
City council sets aside land around the Glenmore Reservoir for a park.

APRIL 28, 1957
The Southern Alberta Jubilee Auditorium opens.

SEPT. 3, 1957
The Social Credit government gives a $20 oil dividend to every Alberta citizen.

MARCH 1959
Calgary's population sits near 220,000.

JUNE 18, 1959
Ernest Manning's Social Credit Party wins a seventh consecutive majority.

JULY 9, 1959
Queen Elizabeth and Prince Philip visit the city.

Canwest Archive, Agata Urbaniak, Peter Suneson, and Calgary Herald Archive

1950s

The dream started in a dusty field, about a half-mile south of town. Save for the chirping of a few crickets, the air was still. The first star of the night twinkled in the sweeping prairie sky. To the west, the Rockies faded from purple to grey, as the sun slipped behind them.

Headlights of vehicles cut through the dusk, as a small line of cars made its way from Calgary towards the field. Western Canada's first drive-in theatre was about to open. It was May 12, 1949, and it was opening night at the Chinook Drive-In Theatre.

This drive-in would change the face of entertainment in the area for years to come. More importantly, however, it would lead to a dream — the dream of creating Chinook Centre, a development that has helped shape the city of Calgary for five decades and continues to do so today.

When the Chinook Drive-In opened, the Second World War had ended just a few years earlier. Cities across North America were moving from an era of difficulty and despair into an age of innovation and optimism. Inventions burst forward in every field imaginable. A new device called a "stored-program computer" began operation. The first 45-rpm records were introduced. And an awe-inspiring contraption called a Polaroid camera sold for a whopping $89.95.

At the same time, the drive-in theatre was becoming an entertainment phenomenon. Created by a guy from New Jersey who nailed a bed-sheet screen to trees in his backyard in 1932, the concept was emerging as the ultimate family diversion.

Five Calgary businessmen knew a good idea when they heard it and decided to bring the drive-in to town. Mervyn (Red) Dutton, Reg Jennings, Frank Kershaw, Harold Millican and Ross Henderson established Western Drive-In Theatres Ltd., with Chinook being their initial drive-in project and one of the first in Canada.

BY THE NUMBERS

DRIVE-IN THEATRES
- The drive-in theatre was created in 1932.
- By 1948, there were more than 800 in North America.
- Western Canada's first was Chinook Drive-In, in Calgary.
- Drive-in numbers peaked at close to 5,000 in 1958.
- Today, there are an estimated 450 drive-ins still operating in North America.

The Chinook Drive-In, the precursor to Chinook Shopping Centre, was Western Canada's first drive-in when it opened in May 1949.   *Photo courtesy Trudy Selmser*
Below: Mr. Peanut attends a promotional event at the drive-in.

When Chinook Drive-In opened in 1949, there were about 1,000 drive-ins in North America. That number soared to almost 5,000 in less than 10 years.

The ownership group told the local press in 1949 that the $160,000 project was built in record time — eight weeks.

In one newspaper article, drive-in neophytes received a quick primer on how the outdoor theatre would work: "Each car will have its own loud speaker with volume control. When ready to leave, cars will move forward on the sloping ramp, turn left on the lane behind the next row of cars and leave by a wide exit road."

The movie playing on Chinook's opening night was Perils of Pauline, with The Count of Monte Cristo taking the big screen the following week. Admission to Chinook was only 60 cents, while children under 12 were admitted free.

Telling of the times were the newspaper ads used to lure Calgarians south of city limits to the drive-in. One ad told people: "Smoke if you like! You can't annoy anybody!" Other promotional lures included, "No babysitters; save the cost," and "Don't dress up! Come as you are."

Calgarians came not only for the movie, but also because the drive-in was a fam-

Above: Ads appeared in the Calgary Herald for the drive-in's opening May 12 (left) and on May 16 (right) in 1949, enticing Calgarians to visit.
Left: Drive-in manager Ken McGregor (pictured) quickly realized the value of marketing, as seen in this promotion for Francis the Talking Mule.
Lorne Burkell photo; courtesy Don McGregor

NOW . . .

. . . AND THEN

The 1950s brought a number of changes to Calgary, including construction of the city's first skyscraper in the 600 block of 8th Avenue S.W. The Barron Building was built at a cost of $1,125,000. Original tenants in the 11-storey building included Sun Oil, Shell and TransCanada Pipelines, along with the Uptown Theatre. Today, the building and theatre still stand. Interior and exterior renovations are planned for the near future to restore the building to its former glory.
Top: Grant Black photo
Right: Courtesy the Barrons, Calgary Herald Archive

CONSTRUCTION BY A DYNAMIC DUO

• In 1941, Reg Jennings and Red Dutton formed the Standard Gravel and Surfacing Company. The company's construction projects ranged from roads and pipelines to airports, fire halls and dams.
• Under the Standard name, about 35 other companies sprouted up, with signature projects that included Chinook Centre, McMahon Stadium, the Jubilee Auditoriums in Calgary and Edmonton, and parts of Heritage Park.
• After purchasing an outfit called General Construction Limited, the company became known as Standard General.
• Standard General was sold to BACM Industries in 1968, the first in a string of ownership changes. The company still operates today.

ily outing. Playgrounds, train rides and even carousels at drive-ins kept children entertained before the show started.

Visiting the concession stand was also a key part of the drive-in ritual. On-screen promos reminded people to take "time out for a delicious snack in the sparkling refreshment building."

Those unforgettable promos — featuring dancing hot dogs, pirouetting cups of pop and marching ice cream treats — became legendary in popular culture.

"The war was over, the economy was starting to explode and the drive-in was the place to be for families," says Donald McGregor, whose father Ken honed his promotional and management skills at the Chinook and Cinema Park drive-

ins, before becoming Chinook Centre's first mall manager.

The opening of the Chinook Drive-In Theatre brought together the people, the land and the ideas that would eventually lead to the development of Calgary's largest shopping centre. Step one was complete.

As the 1950s drew to a close, drive-in theatres declined in popularity. Society was changing and so were people's entertainment choices. In 1957 — the year that rumours surfaced about a plan to build a massive shopping centre in south Calgary — the Cold War was heating up, as was the Cuban Revolution. The Soviet Union sent the first animal into space — a dog named Laika. The year also saw

Sign of the times: A group of children received free cap guns at the Gene Autry night at the Chinook Drive-In, which became known for its special events in Calgary during the 1950s.   Courtesy Don McGregor

Mervyn (Red) Dutton, an extroverted leader, partnered with Reg Jennings to create Chinook.

the debut of the Frisbee, the pacemaker and the Cat in the Hat from Dr. Seuss.

The biggest change, however, was the dramatic rise of television's popularity. New TV shows were debuting every month, including Leave It To Beaver and Front Page Challenge, while programs such as Candid Camera, Howdy Doody, Dragnet and Truth or Consequences were ongoing favourites. Creating the largest stir on the small screen was Elvis Presley, making his third appearance on The Ed Sullivan Show in 1957. Even while performing a gospel number, Peace In The Valley, Elvis was only televised from the waist up.

When Chinook Drive-In opened, there were only about two million television sets in North America. By the time its closure was announced in the late 1950s, that number skyrocketed to more than 41 million (of which 150,000 were colour sets.) An increasing number of people were staying at home and making television their preferred entertainment choice.

Drive-in numbers dwindled. The year 1958 had been the height of the drive-in's popularity, but within five years there were almost 1,000 fewer outdoor screens in North America. The owners of Chinook, however, were visionaries and they quietly began discussing new options before the decline began.

They were always on the lookout for the

next opportunity and the next big thing. Three of them — Red Dutton, Reg Jennings and Frank Kershaw — had an inkling what that next big thing would be: the shopping centre.

"Just as the automobile helped revolutionize the theatre industry, so is the private passenger car revolutionizing commerce," Kershaw said in an interview with Calgary Herald writer Merv Anderson in the late 1950s. "The motoring public wants handy parking facilities and one-stop shopping."

When the triumvirate of Kershaw, Dutton and Jennings began planning a new shopping centre at the location of the Chinook Drive-In, observers speculated it was destined for success. Each man exhibited drive, determination and the entrepreneurial spirit that is both expected and valued in Calgary.

Kershaw, mild mannered and hard working, was known as a pioneer in Canada's theatre business. His father had opened a silent movie house in 1913 in Winnipeg, where Kershaw worked as an usher. Eventually becoming a theatre manager, he soon moved to become an executive with the Famous Players chain, overseeing movie houses in Ontario, Manitoba, Saskatchewan and Alberta.

"In the entertainment business you have to keep moving or get left behind," he said in 1959.

In addition to Chinook, Reg Jennings was key in developing other projects, such as Heritage Park.

Frank H. Kershaw used his theatre experience and business sense to become a Chinook partner.

Red Dutton and business partner Reg Jennings were prominent industry leaders in the city. Dutton, left, is pictured here at the annual Stampede Garden Party hosted at his Elbow Drive home. Also shown is his wife, Mrs. M. Dutton, along with his brother and sister-in-law, Mr. and Mrs. R.A. Dutton of California.   Calgary Herald Archive

CALGARY IN THE 1950s

• Calgary's last street car makes its final run to Ogden in 1956.
• Liquor laws change in 1958 and for the first time, Calgarians can enjoy an alcoholic beverage with a meal at hotels.
• In 1953, it becomes legal for bingo to be played, as long as proceeds go to religious or charitable organizations.

Dutton, meanwhile, could best be described as a force of nature. He'd found success as a professional hockey player, a coach, president of the National Hockey League, Hall of Fame inductee and a businessman. His accomplishments seem even more remarkable when put in the context of his personal story.

During the First World War, Dutton lied about his age, enlisted at 16, and after three years of action in France, worked his way up to the rank of sergeant. However, he was injured at Vimy Ridge when 26 pieces of shrapnel shredded parts of his legs and one hip. He waited in a ditch for three days before medical help was available and it was six days until surgeons could properly examine the injuries. They wanted to amputate his right leg. That's when "I learned that hollering pays off," Dutton said years later.

Dutton refused the amputation and vowed that he would walk again. After an 18-month rehabilitation, Dutton walked out of the hospital. Back home in Canada, he spent up to seven hours a day on skates, to further strengthen his legs. Those skating skills, along with a lot of grit and fortitude, eventually led him to play 15 professional seasons with several hockey teams including the Calgary Tigers. While taking on subsequent coaching roles and high-profile positions within the NHL, Dutton also ran a contracting business, following in the footsteps of his father.

"Let's give hockey fair credit," said Dutton, a red-headed extrovert, who'd always been penalty-prone in the game. "Everything I have I owe to hockey," he noted, while being interviewed in 1960. "I was stony broke twice and both times the game gave me a fresh start. It still offers opportunity to young Canadians."

THEN . . .

This view of 8th Avenue, looking west, provides a quick snapshot of Calgary's downtown in the early 1950s. The street is now a pedestrian mall.   *Calgary Herald Archive*

While business fortunes smiled on Dutton, life wasn't always easy. He lost two of his three sons in the Second World War, while steadfastly continuing to build his company and community. Dutton took on roles including president of the Calgary Exhibition and Stampede, potentate of the Al Azhar Shriners Temple and president of the Calgary Stampeders football club, while also donating time and money to recreational hockey rinks, parks, cancer research and hospitals.

Dutton formed a long-lasting association with Reg Jennings years before Chinook Centre or the Chinook Drive-in was planned. If it was Dutton bringing the physical energy to the partnership, it was Jennings who brought calm efficiency. "He's our brain," Dutton said of Jennings.

Long before the idea of the shopping centre took hold, Dutton and Jennings

. . . AND NOW

Grant Black photo

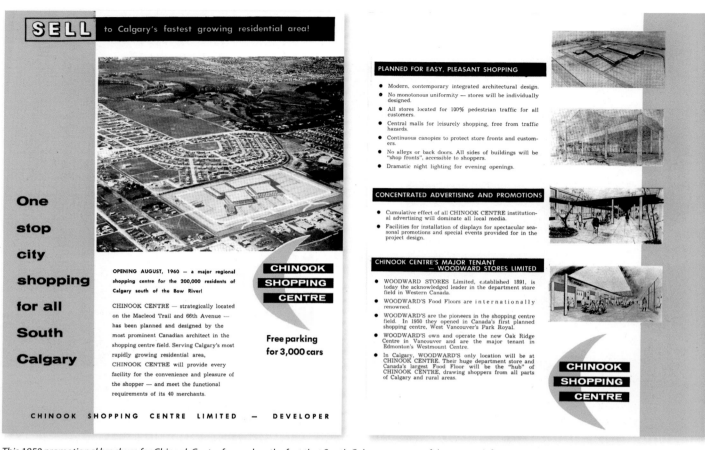

This 1958 promotional brochure for Chinook Centre focused on the fact that South Calgary was one of the country's fastest growing areas.   *Courtesy Glenbow Archives*

had been working together as a dynamic duo, of sorts, changing the landscape of western Canada with projects of all scopes and sizes. Forming Standard Gravel and Surfacing Company, and several subsidiaries, the pair built office buildings, industrial plants, highways, airports, and oil and gas pipelines.

"He (Reg Jennings) had great vision," says Amy Jennings, who is married to Reg's son, Roy. "He had the foresight to see what was coming in business."

Jennings was also extremely community minded and was instrumental in developing Heritage Park. He helped the park acquire the land it needed when the park was proposed, and his company paid the foreman who oversaw the park's construction, Roy Jennings notes.

Jennings' and Dutton's contrasting business styles helped propel Standard to become one of Canada's most respected

businesses. "Red would barge in breaking the china and Reg would come along and put it together," one of their colleagues said at the time.

By 1960, Standard had grown to include 24 companies and was awarded about $70 million in contracts that year alone. The two men's reputation as impeccable contractors and businessmen was cemented by their work on more than 22 airports, the Jubilee auditoriums in Calgary and Edmonton, McMahon Stadium and a 400-kilometre stretch of road through the muskeg between northern Alberta and the Northwest Territories.

The pair's 40-year-plus partnership was sealed with only a handshake. "We've been partners for 44 years and we've never had a quarrel," Dutton noted of his friend Jennings.

The men who would oversee the development of Chinook Centre were now

ready to undertake one of their biggest challenges. The city was prepared for it, too. The lean years of the Depression were fading into the past. War-time shortages of homes, cars and building materials were finally easing. And, importantly, the Leduc No. 1 well blew in 1947, causing the city's energy business to flourish. Oil exploration grew, and so did oil finds. Alberta's economic driver shifted from agriculture to oil and gas.

"Business in Calgary has averaged higher during 1951 than for any other year in local history," a Herald story reported at the end of that year. "At present, general activity is topping 12 months ago by a spectacular 21 per cent."

Throughout the 1950s, Calgary began to feel more like a city than a town.

In addition to the blizzards, Chinook winds, floods, accidents, flu epidemic and polio outbreaks that made the news, Calgary also began facing big city issues.

The construction of Chinook Shopping Centre reflected a North American trend of retail moving away from downtown cores.

Courtesy Chinook Centre

Two hundred beer waiters went on strike for a month. Night spots increased their admission charges from $2.50 to $5 per couple and $12 to $15 for special events like New Year's Eve. Bread prices rose by one cent to 16 cents a loaf in 1952, while bus fares increased from 10 cents to 15 cents a few years later. Calgarians also voted overwhelmingly to approve the serving of mixed drinks in city parlours, much to the public disappointment of Premier Ernest Manning.

A 1957 Calgary Herald series examined how the city saw itself. One old-timer explained it this way: "Calgary's structures, ideals and objectives have changed. This is no longer a small 'big town.' There is the rush and bustle of big business. It's become a professional operation. . . . It brings a great strangeness for those who have lived here some time."

Writer Bob Shiels noted that "Calgary, rightly or wrongly, is known as a high-living, free-spending city where telephones jangle, horns honk, money is spent and big decisions are made to a greater extent and on a larger scale than in most other cities, particularly on the prairies."

Mayor Don Mackay held Calgary's top post from 1950-59, steering the city through this time of growth and also ensuring Calgary didn't lose its identity along the way. He promoted the concept of the white cowboy hat as a symbol of the city, presenting them to visiting dignitaries at every opportunity.

At the time, there were 25,000 owner-occupied homes in the city, 16,000 apartments and 4,500 homeowners who took in lodgers. Telephones numbered 82,623 and for those interested in spicing up their home décor, phones were now available in colours other than black.

Anybody who was anybody was purchasing a vehicle and the car was king. The increase in mobility led to an increase in urban spread.

The city got bigger and neighbourhoods began being built farther away from the downtown core. Modest neighbourhood shopping centres began springing up, often anchored by a grocery store.

Woodward's To Build Shopping Centre Here

Hays' Site Chosen

By HERB SURPLIS

NEW SHOPPING CENTRE. This is a photograph of the same type of shopping centre which is to be erected on the site of the Hays Farm...

Asiatic 'Flu In City, Dr. W.H. Hill Believes

Hospital Heads Issue Appeal For Caution

By JOHN TAYLOR

STORM BURIES MONTANA IN 14-INCH SNOWFALL

COLD WEATHER CASUALTIES.

Hutterites Are Given Three Weeks To Leave

Wardlow Ranchers Told Sect Forced To Leave V-Bar-V Ranch

Air Crash Victim Identi...

Integration Issue Goes Court

Russia Blames West ... East Unrest

Truckers, Buses Gear To Offset Rail Strike

Parley Turned Down

FLOODS HIT OIL FIELD.

Woodward Shopping Park Slated For Macleod Trail

Initial Cost Of Project $6,500,000

By MERV ANDERSON

ill Site Picked or Vendors

OW HELPS FARMERS T HIGHWAY CREWS

s July End Session

Gas Firm Denies Plotting

BAROMETER BETTY Says
CLOUDY
Low 30, High 55

All-Out For Red Support
Dulles Bid Hints Cut In Arctic H-Flights

By J. A. WALKER

ALBERTA ASKS NORTHERN LINE

Craigmyle Hi... R... S...

PRESS RELEASE

Authorized by Chinook Shopping Centre Limited

For Publication on Saturday, May 3rd 1958

It was announced today that early in 1961 Woodward Sto... Limited will open a complete department store and food market in a new major shopping centre which will be located on the West Side of the Macleod Trail between 61st and 66th Avenues including the properties now occupied by the Chinook Drive-In Theatre and the Skyline Restaurant.

The new Shopping Centre will be developed and wholly owned by Chinook Shopping Centre Limited, a newly formed Calgary company, which will be closely associated with Standard Holdings Limited, a well known local company. Principals of Chinook Shopping Centre Limited include Mr. Mervyn (Red) Dutton and Mr. R.F. Jennings, prominent city businessmen and contractors, and Mr. F.H. Kershaw, general manager of Western Drive-In Theatres Ltd.

The new centre, which will have parking facilities for up to 3,000 automobiles, will be located on an area of approximately 40 acres and there will be a total of 400,000 square feet or more of retail space available and leading independent Calgary merchants will be invited and given priority for space in this locally inspired project.

The shopping centre, which will serve the rapidly expanding population in the Southern section of the city, when fully developed will be one of the largest regional centres in Canada and the estimated cost is expected to exceed $8,000,000.00. In addition to the large Woodwards

---

Above: Newspapers were abuzz over the announcement of a planned shopping centre. Below: Archived material shows Chinook Centre's first press release was distributed May 1958, and that its stock offering held the promise of future financial success.

On Feb. 23, 1959, looking south from the mall site, only a few homes existed where Glenmore Trail and massive development are now located. Courtesy Al Hardstaff

As the city spread out, so did shopping areas in far-flung city neighbourhoods, says Robert M. Stamp in the book Suburban Modern-Postwar Dreams in Calgary. Stamp recalls a telling quote from Frank Cox, an American development consultant, who spoke at a 1953 meeting of the Calgary Chamber of Commerce: "Calgary within the next 10 years can expect a shift in retail buying from the downtown area to the bright new shopping districts in the suburbs."

Cox noted there was a new breed of retail store on the horizon featuring new design and "glamourous exteriors to catch the eye, superior interior lighting and store fixtures, and wide aisles to accommodate customers."

Other retail changes would include background music in stores and trained personnel, ready to wait on shoppers. Once established, these stores will "rip the shingles off" many downtown businesses, he predicted.

In 1958, Simpsons-Sears North Hill at the corner of 16th Avenue and 14th Street N.W. opened, becoming Calgary's first regional shopping centre. The biggest change in Calgary shopping, however, was yet to come.

When the Chinook Centre proposal was announced, it quickly became the talk of the town. In September 1957, Woodward's confirmed it would build a store in Calgary, using 40 acres of space on the Hays farm for a shopping centre development.

"We believe that the phenomenal growth of Calgary will continue and will take place mainly in south Calgary," said Charles N. (Chunky) Woodward, president and general manager of his family company.

The shopping centre, 40 to 42 stores anchored by Woodward's, would cost an estimated $10 million to build and be

ONE SWEET DEAL

Details of the proposal to build Chinook Centre:

• Cost would be $8 million to $10 million;
• The site was 40 acres in size;
• Free parking for 3,000 to 3,500 vehicles would be available;
• Woodward's would be the focal point of the mall;
• 40 other stores would also open;
• 1,500 jobs would exist at the centre.

Henry Liebelt, construction worker on the original mall:

"I worked on the cement pour and it was quite a building to work on. . . . The Palliser Hotel had been one of the biggest buildings in town before Chinook, but when Chinook came along most people hadn't seen anything like it."

Cindy Liebelt, long-time Chinook customer:

"I met my husband in 1956, and one of our first dates was at the Chinook Drive-In Theatre. . . . We shared our first kiss on the site of what is now Chapters bookstore. . . . I remember piling our little ones in our baby buggy and walking down the gravel road that was Glenmore Trail for the grand opening of Chinook. Woodward's handed out roses. . . . We have been married for 51 years now and live a short bus ride from Chinook. It is our major shopping destination and the home of our favourite shops and restaurants." Chinook also provided the family with a local library branch, the annual tradition of attending the Stampede Breakfast and part-time jobs for the Liebelt children when they were teens. "Chinook has grown and been renovated so many times since the grand opening, and our lives have been intricately woven over the generations. . . . Chinook, what would we do without you?"

Henry and Cindy Liebelt shared their first kiss in 1956 at the Chinook Drive-In, on a spot that is now occupied by the popular Chapters store in Chinook Shopping Centre.   Grant Black photo

Dan Hays, prominent lawyer and former senator:

The area around Chinook Centre was recognized for its "retail" offerings long before Chinook came on the scene, says Hays. Calgary's street car line ended in this area, meaning it was a transportation hub for folks making their way into and out of the city, he recalls. The area was also home to a small store named Humphreys, which was a frequent stop for hardware, grocery items and gas. "It was an oasis between Calgary proper and the countryside. . . . It was a precursor to what would someday develop in this area – Chinook Centre. . . . which grew to become a great mall."

Sue Tersmette, Chinook customer:

"I grew up in Meadowlark Park, the community where Chinook Mall is located, so I saw it grow up as I did, from a couple of stores to the mega-mall that it is now. I remember the days of Loblaws. . . and Kresge's, with its cafeteria-style eating area, with great fries and gravy. . . . I have very fond memories of Woodward's and its dining room where the family went for baked sole on Thursdays after getting groceries. . . . One of the funniest things I remember as a kid was going to the parking lot and playing on the huge piles of snow that had been plowed up along the edge of the parking lot. Those were the days when we had so much more snow in winter and it lasted all winter. . . . One of my first part-time jobs was at Ben Moss. I think I made $3.50 or $4 an hour. If I were to look back on its 50 years, Chinook has always been a big part of my growing up."

Milli Pratt, wife of the late Bill Pratt (above), a prominent Calgarian who oversaw Chinook's early construction:

"When Chinook was built, it was a very good mall. It was really *the* mall. . . . This was very big for the city. Now, Calgary is full of a whole bunch of towers and big buildings, but back then, it was something else. It was a good job. Bill enjoyed it."

The Pioneer

Model SH-4

As plans for Chinook grew, so too did the community that is home to the centre. These sketches show a blueprint for a typical home constructed in Meadowlark Park.
Courtesy Meadowlark Park Community Association

This striking new design, featured in the Calgary Housebuilders' Association show of 1954, has rapidly become one of the most popular of the Art Sullivan Homes.

Similar in many ways to the larger "Super Pioneer," it gives you many of the advantages of the bigger home, but at a considerable reduction in price. The three bedrooms, with high windows allowing free placement of furniture, the two bathrooms, and large living-dining room combination, assure you of the spacious living you need.

Unusually large closet space
island bar

KITCHEN 12' x 11'

BEDROOM 12' 6" x 12'

DINING AREA

BEDROOM 9' 6" x 9'

BEDROOM 10' x 9'

LIVING ROOM 24' 6" x 18

THE MEADOWLARK

STYLE

1:304

an ART SULLIVAN HOME

the focal point of a $75-million to $100-million residential and industrial area planned by Kelwood Corporation. This initial proposal suggested the mall sit further south than its eventual location.

City Hall Commissioner Dudley E. Batchelor hailed the announcement as good news for Calgary. "The development will provide a big boost to the economy of the city. It will create many jobs in the construction field and will later provide permanent employment for a large number of citizens."

The project was well received, but as it moved through the development process, plans were slightly altered, specifically in regards to its location. Red Dutton, Reg Jennings and Frank Kershaw were ready to close their Chinook Drive-In and wanted to build the new shopping centre on that site.

The men's newly formed company — Chinook Shopping Centre Ltd. — convinced Woodward's to change its planned location and then announced it would be the company moving ahead with the project on Macleod Trail, between 61st and 66th Avenues. The project was a revision of the 1957 plan for Haysboro, but "better parking facilities at the new site helped to dictate the change," local newspapers reported. The developers also noted that traffic studies indicated this second site was more accessible for Calgarians.

When the owners set their sights on building Calgary's greatest mall, the sky was the limit. A 1950s pamphlet on the mall said, "Chinook Centre will provide every facility for the convenience and pleasure of the shopper — and meet the functional requirements of its 40 merchants."

RETAIL SPENDING

• The average Calgarian had $1,487 of disposable income in the year 1959; $600 of that was spent on retail goods.
• Chinook Centre owners predicted people living within two miles of the centre would spend $240 at the mall annually.
• Those within four miles of Chinook were expected to spend $120 each year.

This 1959 construction photo of Chinook shows south Calgary was becoming home to a few other businesses, such as Maclin Ford.   *Courtesy Al Hardstaff*

Selling points throughout the pamphlet noted there would be free parking for 3,000 cars on the 40-acre site and that it would feature "modern, contemporary integrated architectural design." The mall was designed as an open-air concept. (The covered ceiling for the entire mall would be built five years after the 1960 opening.)

Cost estimates ranged from $6.5 million to $10 million, with the developers hoping to complete the project with $8 million. When the mall was fully operational, it was expected to employ 1,500 people.

"The shopping centre, which will serve the rapidly expanding population in the southern section of the city, when fully developed will be one of the largest regional centres in Canada," the developers said in the first ever Chinook Shopping Centre press release.

"With a Western organization like Woodward Stores acting as the hub and with leading local and national mer-

chants included, this new shopping centre will undoubtedly be an unqualified success and a valuable asset to our city," Reg Jennings, general manager of Standard Holdings Limited, said at the time in 1958.

Construction was scheduled to commence early in 1959 and it was expected that occupancy would occur in 1961. The mall was off to a great start, however, with construction starting sooner than expected in September 1958. Work began on the first phase, which included Woodward's and 40 smaller stores. Woodward's was slated to be about 240,000 square feet in size, over two floors. Its Food Floor, approximately 50,000 square feet in size, would be the largest in the country.

As plans for the store moved forward, company president Chunky Woodward talked to newspapers about the development. At age 32 in 1958, Woodward was often called "Canada's youngest merchant prince." He revealed that he originally planned to begin building a

store in Calgary sometime in the 1960s, but started sooner after inspecting the city and hearing its growth statistics.

"South Calgary is one of the fastest growing areas in the West," the Calgary Herald reported at the time. "Present indications are that the city may expand 10 miles south to Midnapore on Macleod Trail. Plans have been blueprinted to build homes in the south end for 175,000 persons by 1978. . . . With that rate of growth, the (Woodward's) president believes the company can't go wrong in making an early start."

From its inception, the developers thought of Chinook Shopping Centre as a city within a city. Not only would it include shopping, dining and entertainment amenities, it would also house banks, doctor offices and service outlets where you could do everything from get shoes repaired to renew a driver's licence. Already thinking big, the developers noted second and third phases

The city boasted ample room for development, looking southeast from the Chinook site. Macleod Trail stretches across the top of this 1958 photo. Courtesy Al Hardstaff

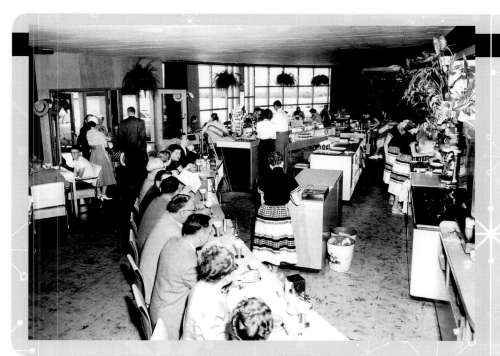

SLICE OF LIFE

The Skyline Restaurant, pictured here in 1951, was a popular diner located near the Chinook Centre site. It eventually became a pancake house, but years earlier was known for hosting bands, such as the Nite Hawks, seen below performing a live set for radio station CKXL.

Photos courtesy Meadowlark Park Community Association

An artist's rendering of Chinook Centre graced the front of this invitation to a VIP pre-opening day reception at the Palliser Hotel.   *Courtesy Roy & Amy Jennings*

could include a hotel, a library and a 200-bed hospital, which would take construction costs to $15 million.

It was the suggestion of a hospital that stirred the most public debate, especially as Calgarians wondered who would pay for it. "Officials said no firm plans have been completed for financing of the proposed hospital," according to news reports at the time.

"It may be that the municipal, provincial and federal governments will be invited in, or it may be a strictly private hospital to tie up with a medical centre," a Chinook official noted in the press. "We are wide open for negotiations."

Echoing a refrain still heard in the 21st century, Mayor Don Mackay welcomed the proposal and said: "The hospital could play a significant role in relieving the hospital bed shortage in the city." He added that the Chinook Centre plans appeared to be going "far beyond the normal concept of centre projects."

In the end, the idea of building a hospital at Chinook never materialized; however, a medical office tower did. Dutton's and Jennings' company also participated in constructing the Rockyview General Hospital in south Calgary.

From a business perspective, there were many reasons why local entrepreneurs were attracted to Chinook Centre. Calgary was the fastest growing city in Canada, with an annual population rate increase of eight per cent. From 1948 to 1958, the city had grown from 113,718 people to around 220,000.

"Growth potential (is) unlimited," noted a 1950s pamphlet, highlighting reasons why merchants should consider setting up shop in Chinook. "The residential development of Calgary is pushing straight south. The southern portion of the city has practically no barriers to restrict this expansion."

The idea of a shopping centre was still a new concept to Calgary. The Simpsons-Sears North Hill shopping centre had opened in 1958, making it the city's first mall, but plans for Chinook were on a much larger scale. Chinook was touted to be "complete one-stop shopping."

The business acumen of Chinook's ownership group was obvious from the start. They weren't about to build a shopping centre and hope people would come. There was a detailed marketing plan they relied on, complete with research that showed how much money was out there to be spent.

Despite the fact that it was still in the

early days of advertising and marketing, Chinook's owners knew their importance. One promotional brochure said, "The cumulative effect of all Chinook Centre institutional advertising will dominate all local media."

Construction of Chinook sped ahead. In August 1958, the city recommended acceptance of the developers' offer of $15,000 for a portion of a roadway allowance on 61st Avenue (Macleod Trail and Meadowview Road) that was 66 feet wide and 1,000 feet in length. Mayor Don Mackay objected on the grounds that the price was too high, but Ald. J.J. Hanna argued the sale price worked out to the equivalent of about $1,500 per city lot, which was less than the average lot price most people were paying. "We're not robbing these people," Hanna said.

The next month, the Chinook Drive-In Theatre closed its gates, with demolition starting the following Monday.

Within days, the official sod-turning ceremony for the shopping centre was scheduled. Dignitaries, including Chunky Woodward, were to arrive in Calgary for the event on Sept. 19, 1958, but the weather wreaked havoc. When Woodward attempted to leave Vancouver for Calgary that morning, the

The sod-turning ceremony for Chinook Centre was a windy affair. Pictured are (from left) Mayor Don Mackay; Reg Jennings; Charles (Chunky) Woodward; Mervyn (Red) Dutton; A.H. Williamson (Director Woodward's and Wood Gundy Co.); G.D. Glanville (Woodward's Vice-president); R.N. Bligh (Woodward's development manager); and T.K. Campbell (Vice-president, Woodward's Edmonton stores.)

Calgary Herald Archive; courtesy Roy Jennings

de-icing equipment on his scheduled TCA plane malfunctioned. An elegant 1 p.m. luncheon at the Palliser Hotel, meant to celebrate the occasion of the sod-turning, was cancelled. Woodward and a handful of his company's Vancouver-based managers were transferred to the next available flight to Calgary, but that flight was running late.

The noon sod-turning was postponed to 4 p.m. to await the Vancouver group's arrival, but the weather had one more trick to play. The drive-in theatre's screen was scheduled to be toppled over, as Woodward dug out the first shovel full of dirt for the new centre. The wind, however, was growing stronger throughout the day

and eventually blew over the partially-dismantled screen before the official ceremony and sod turning occurred.

Despite the wind and a rainstorm, spirits were high. Woodward stood, smiling and surveying the site, before plunging a shovel into the ground. The shovel itself was a significant symbol of the day. It was a $1.49 spade, which had been used to turn the sod for his family's department stores across Western Canada since 1952, a tradition started by Woodward's late father.

At the ceremony, Red Dutton promised the construction would be one of the fastest completions of a major shopping centre in Canada's history, according to

the now-defunct Albertan newspaper.

"This centre is scheduled to be open in August 1960, and believe me, it's going to be all finished and occupied by that time," Dutton said.

The Albertan noted that Woodward indicated the project "would be the first one of its size conceived and arranged for entirely in Western Canada. . . . It was an indication of what Westerners could do when they joined forces."

Mayor Mackay presented each of the developers and Vancouver visitors with a white hat. Although the wind blew, the hats held steady, a symbol of what Calgarians have always valued — hard work, big dreams and optimism.

The Year Was 1960 . . .

In the same year that Chinook Centre opened its doors, the entire continent experienced a period of development and discovery. Here are just a few of the crazes and creations that influenced North American society in 1960.

- Single-serving ketchup packets are introduced, as are drinks in aluminum cans, Granny Smith apples and Domino's Pizza.

- About 60 per cent of North Americans own their own home; many households have cars and washing machines; and, about 90 per cent possess at least one TV set.

- Chubby Checker creates a dance craze with The Twist. Sergeant Elvis Presley receives an honorable discharge after two years in the army on March 23, 1960. The Quarrymen, a rock and roll band from Liverpool, change their name to The Beatles and the world is never the same.

  Electronic watches and lasers are invented. The first touch-tone telephones are tested with 10 buttons, rather than the 12 buttons seen today.

  Xerox introduces the first commercial "document reproduction machine," known today as the photocopier. The first contraceptive drug, the Pill, becomes available – to married women only.

- The top three songs of the year are Will You Love Me Tomorrow by the Shirelles; Georgia On My Mind by Ray Charles; and Only The Lonely by Roy Orbison. Itsy Bitsy Teenie Weenie Yellow Polka Dot Bikini is also recorded.

- Artist Andy Warhol paints his creation Campbell Soup Can, Tomato and Rice. Hallmark introduces the first Peanuts greeting card.

- Top movies include Spartacus, The Magnificent Seven and Psycho from Alfred Hitchcock. The Flintstones, Coronation Street, My Three Sons and The Andy Griffith Show debut on television. The book Lady Chatterley's Lover by D.H. Lawrence is banned in Canada.

- The average North American income is $5,315 US. A two-door Ford Mustang hard top costs $2,368. An automatic can opener is $8.88.

OPENING DAY

The ancient Greeks used the word "agora" when describing shopping centres of their day. An agora was the marketplace where people gathered for trade, business, pleasure and conversation. In 1960, a new agora was about to open in Calgary — Chinook Shopping Centre.

"Chinook changed people's shopping habits; it became the place to go, for everyone," says Roy Jennings, son of Chinook founder Reg Jennings. "There was really a need for growth in retail and in business . . . and Chinook provided that growth."

As opening day — Aug. 17, 1960 — approached for Chinook Shopping Centre, buzz grew across the city. While Calgary's first shopping centre, North Hill, had opened in 1958, Chinook promised to be bigger and better. Curiosity was at a fever pitch. Local newspapers regularly reported on construction progress, new retailers and proposed innovations.

"Many new features (are) promised," trumpeted one article. It highlighted a vast parking lot for 3,000 to 3,500 cars that would be well lit and paved. The mall's size, at 440,000-plus square feet, would be the city's largest. And, a conveyor belt for parcel pick-up at Woodward's was becoming the talk of the town. It would move shoppers' groceries from the Food Floor to a convenient pick-up station in the parking lot. "This is a relatively new feature in Canadian shopping centres," with only Vancouver and Montreal having similar pick-ups in the entire country, the article said.

Excitement grew when Chinook Centre announced it would remain open two nights a week — the first centre in Western Canada to offer a second night of shopping for customers. At a time when retail was still largely a 9 a.m. to 6 p.m., Tuesday to Saturday venture, increased night shopping was a significant development.

BY THE NUMBERS

CHINOOK CENTRE'S OPENING DAY
- **45:** Number of stores and services.
- **1,000:** Employees at Chinook Centre in an average week.
- **1,800:** Employees during peak periods.
- **481,053:** Square footage of total building area (all floors.)
- **12.5 million:** Dollars required to complete Chinook Centre.
- **4:** Number of landscaped acres at the centre.
- **21,560:** Number of light bulbs in use at Chinook.
- **3,000:** Number of plants and trees in the mall; enough for 100 or more private homes.

Amy and Roy Jennings watched Chinook Centre grow from the ground up, as Roy's father – Reg Jennings – was one of its founders.   Grant Black photo

The announcement was made after the centre's merchants met in the banquet rooms of the Carolina restaurant, an early foreshadowing of two themes that would help define Chinook. Firstly, the Carolina would become a key gathering place for many members of the Chinook community. Secondly, at this meeting the shop owners formally organized the Chinook Merchants' Association — a group that helped promote the centre and became the backbone of many Chinook operations and events.

From the start, Chinook Centre was more than a group of retailers renting adjacent spaces. It was a community where all stakeholders had equal interest and involvement in ensuring the centre's success. Nowhere was this more apparent than in the Chinook Merchants' Association. The association united all businesses in the centre for discussion of policy and promotional matters. Each merchant had an equal voice at the table, regardless of the size of his store or business. The promotion and achievements of Chinook Shopping Centre were shared by all. It contributed to the sense of family that was growing among community members.

"The Merchants' Association was an opportunity from the mall owners to give the tenants a say," says Al Hardstaff, the former owner of Chinook Optical who worked in the mall for 47 years. "Plus, it helped merchants get to know each other and talk about common concerns. It helped build the Chinook community. It was an honour to be on the (association's) board. It had a real spirit."

While the Merchants' Association was

This August 1960 aerial photo shows Chinook Centre's 3,000-plus parking spots. Macleod Trail runs from the bottom of the photo to the right.   *Calgary Herald Archive*

Chinook's opening was the talk of the town, as seen in this 1960 advertising supplement.

MEMORABLE MOMENTS

Trudy Kung, former model:
"Being part of the fashion shows during opening week was very exciting," says Kung who modelled in Europe for the House of Dior before moving to Calgary in the 1950s. "At the time, it seemed we had more beautiful clothes than we have now. There were more boutiques that were very nice; the fashions were lovely. We were very excited. . . . Woodward's was the highlight of the mall. The employees there were friendly and they tried to keep customers happy. All in all, it was a very nice experience."

Betty Flock, Chinook customer and shop owner:
"Opening day at Chinook Centre, (there were) hordes of people, all ages. My girlfriend Barb Gyles and myself decided to attend with our children in tow, her six and my five, all under 10, pushing strollers, holding hands, (with) lots of threats of 'Don't get lost.' Waiting for the doors to open was exciting. (We were) chatting with everyone, like we had known each other forever. Then the influx of humanity pouring through the doors was amazing. (It was) a day to remember," says Flock. Later in the 1960s, Flock opened the Mais Oui boutique in Southridge Mall, which ultimately became part of Chinook Centre.

TEMPT YOUR TASTE BUDS

Chinook Centre's food outlets and restaurants offered a variety of specials on opening day:
• Kresge's lunch counter featured a turkey dinner for 60 cents, a salad plate for 55 cents and a slice of fresh apple pie for 15 cents;
• Nut House specials included peanut brittle at 44 cents a pound and orange or lemon fruit slices at 29 cents a pound;
• At Woodward's Food Floor, two pounds of bananas were selling for 25 cents, one pound of coffee for 49 cents and three pints of ice cream for 39 cents;
• The Patricia Bakery was offering a dozen crusty rolls for 24 cents or a chiffon pie for 44 cents.
• At Save-On Meats, a T-bone or sirloin steak was advertised at 69 cents.

Julie Ferguson, Chinook customer:
"I was 10 years old when Chinook Centre opened. My mother took my twin sister and me, in our Sunday best, to the opening day. What a thrill! . . . I don't remember a lot about the actual stores except Woodward's. It was the best. I remember thinking, 'How will a store that is so far south make it?'"

excited about the final countdown to opening day, the neighbouring community of Meadowlark Park was feeling a bit uneasy. The pace of construction picked up and Meadowlark Park, to the west of the mall, began expressing growing concerns about traffic and congestion.

Residents presented a 315-signature petition to the City, to discuss traffic problems and safety concerns. Ultimately, the community, Chinook Shopping Centre and the City of Calgary worked together to find solutions to the concerns that were raised. It was the first of several such discussions, which many community residents say evolved into a healthy respect and relationship between Meadowlark Park and the mall today.

At the time, a key benefit for community residents was that one of the country's best food stores was about to become their local grocery store — Woodward's Food Floor. In the 1960s, when international travel was still relatively uncommon, the Food Floor brought global cuisine to many Calgarians for the first time. The fact that this was a made-in-Western-Canada department store only added to its appeal.

"The city was excited; everybody was talking about Woodward's," says Peter de Graaf, former mall organ player and owner of Chinook's Carolina Terrace Restaurant. "Woodward's was a very big thing."

Five weeks before opening, Woodward's president Charles (Chunky) Woodward toured the new space and talked about the store. With a payroll between $2 million and $3 million, staffing numbers would fluctuate between 400 and 900, with the larger number being required during peak retail times, such as Christmas, he said.

High school and university students would be key part-time employees during these busy periods, but at the same time, the chain was seeking "young men and women for responsible (full-time) positions in the company's stores. . . . While a great many employers are insisting today that junior executives have university education, such is not

WOODWARD STORES (Calgary) LTD.
CALGARY - ALBERTA

Parcel Pick Up

An underground conveyor belt carries your food parcels out to the Parcel Pick Up and all you do is drive up and one of the attendants will place your purchases in your car. As many as 35 cars may be serviced at one time.

Auto Service Building.

Fill your car with gas and oil, or have a new muffler installed as well as batteries, tires, and general accessories for your car. You can use Woodward's Charge Account for all your purchases here.

Public Address System

This sound system will provide a pleasant background music for the customers and employees, and will prove most useful in locating mothers of lost children.

Air Conditioning

Woodward's Store is completely Air Conditioned and will allow customers to enjoy their shopping in a most relaxing atmosphere.

Credit Office

Customers may choose from five different credit plans, according to their need. Possibly the most popular will be the "Charge Plate" which, due to a new cash register procedure, will enable the customer to make her purchases as speedily and conveniently as a cash purchase.

****

WOODWARD'S STAFF BENEFITS

. Profit Sharing Plan.	. 5 Day Week
. Staff Shopping Discount.	. Top Remuneration
. Group Insurance.	. Comprehensive Medical Plan and Wage Benefits.
. Group Hospitalization.	
. Recreational Activities.	. Staff Training and Merchandise Courses.

WOODWARD STORES LIMITED

1. Vancouver - Head Office.
2. Edmonton - 101 - 102 Avenue
3. Port Alberni
4. Park Royal Shopping Centre West Vancouver
5. Victoria
6. New Westminster
7. Westmount Shopping Centre - West Edmonton
8. Oakridge Shopping Centre - South Vancouver
9. Chinook Shopping Centre - South Calgary

Woodward's was proud to introduce unique benefits for employees and customers.

WILD ABOUT WOODWARD'S

• The arrival of Woodward's in Calgary in 1960 was front-page news.
• Established in 1891, the Western-Canadian department store chain had stores in Vancouver and Edmonton before Calgary.
• Woodward's opened Canada's first planned shopping centre in West Vancouver's Park Royal in 1950.
• Selling everything from furniture to fashions, Woodward's at Chinook was 236,400 square feet in size, making it the second largest of the chain's nine stores. The Food Floor was an additional 46,100 square feet.
• The Chinook location attracted shoppers from right across the city and the southern half of the province, selling cheeses, spices, gourmet items and seafood that most Albertans had never seen before.
• Woodward's Food Floors were internationally renowned for a high quality of groceries and selection of exotic items, found nowhere else in Western Canada.
• A unique tank containing water mixed from the Pacific and Atlantic oceans was created, so that both crabs and lobsters from opposite coasts could thrive before being sold to consumers.
• Other innovations on the Food Floor included freshly squeezed orange juice, "pizza pies" baked on the spot, a kiddie park, a home economist providing advice and recipes, and a conveyor-belt parcel pick-up.

THEN . . .

Above: Chinook was originally an uncovered mall, which gave rise to 3,000 plants, flowers and trees used to beautify outdoor walkways.
Photo courtesy Roy & Amy Jennings
Right: One of Chinook's comfortable seating areas is located where the above flower bed once sat.
Monica Zurowski photo

. . . AND NOW

the case with Woodward's," local media reported.

Chunky Woodward confirmed the store was looking for all types of good candidates. "It is getting more difficult to get a good job without a university education, but many persons in our company work themselves up regardless of education," he said. "With or without advanced education, we look only for initiative and executive ability."

There was no shortage of applicants. Woodward's announced a benefits program for employees, deemed to be one of the most unique in Canada at the time. In the event of accident or illness, an employee would be paid for six months. That was on top of a profit sharing plan; staff training; merchandise courses; a full comprehensive medical, insurance and hospitalization plan; the best department store wages in Western Canada; and, optional recreational activities.

"They treated you well . . . and it was a fun place to be," says Trudy Selmser, daughter of the first Chinook manager

Ken McGregor and former employee in the Woodward's handbag department. "Woodward's was the place in Calgary to get anything and everything. . . . Even today, people will still make comments about how they bought this or that at Woodward's and how good the quality was."

Woodward's also gained favour with shoppers when they learned of the store's five different credit plans. "Possibly the most popular will be the 'Charge Plate' which, due to a new cash register procedure, will enable the customer to make her purchases as speedily and conveniently as a cash purchase," the store said in company literature.

The company also took great pride in

adhering to the values of the original founder and store from 1891.

"Woodward's became known for the high value it provided to shoppers," says Kip Woodward, son of Chunky Woodward and great grandson of the original founder of the chain. "It was about providing high quality at a good price point."

As Woodward's geared up for the Aug. 17, 1960 grand opening, Ken McGregor was busy ensuring the rest of the mall was ready to open as well. McGregor had proven himself to be a creative and hard-working manager to the Dutton/ Jennings/Kershaw ownership group. He'd managed the Chinook Drive-In and Cinema Park Drive-In, the largest

Chinook Centre's first manager, Ken McGregor, was a marketing whiz. Photo courtesy Don McGregor

outdoor theatre in Western Canada, creating promotions and events that caused a marketing stir across the city.

"He always had ideas," says his son Don, a long-standing business owner himself at Chinook. "He honed his skills as a promoter and learned how to entice audiences in the drive-in business."

One sweet promotion, for example, saw the elder McGregor create lollipop trees for children by organizing a crew to tape hundreds of candies on trees at the drive-in. On another evening, he invited drive-in customers to find a knitting needle in two tons of hay to win a silver tea service. During another event, a cash prize was given to the person who most closely guessed the number of pennies that staff taped to the ceiling of the concession stand — 5,000.

McGregor was now ready to take his ideas and management skills to the next level at Chinook Centre. The ownership group was so impressed with McGregor that they sent him to a shopping centre school in Michigan and on tours of American malls across the United States. He once visited 50 malls between Chicago and Denver, which enabled him to ensure the most modern shopping centre conveniences and ideas were being brought to Chinook.

"Chinook Shopping Centre will definitely rate with any shopping centre in Canada," McGregor told the press as opening day approached. "Chinook is better than the majority of shopping cen-

RECEIVING GUESTS — Mr. and Mrs. C. N. Woodward, far right, of Vancouver, entertained between 500 to 600 guests at a reception Tuesday evening in the Palliser room of the Palliser Hotel. Honored guests who received with them were: (left) Mrs. R. F. Jennings, Mr. Jennings, Mrs. M. A. Dutton and Mr. Dutton. Mrs. Ross Calder is one of the guests shown in the foreground. The occasion marked the completion of the Chinook Shopping Centre on the Macleod Trail.
—Bob Blackmore Photo

tres in the United States and compares favourably with some of the larger ones there. Our concourse here is unique. There's not another like it in all of North America."

McGregor oversaw a flawless opening program, despite a small family crisis. As he entertained dignitaries, his then-14-year-old son Don interrupted the day. The entrepreneurial Don was already cutting his teeth in the shopping centre business with a job in parcel pick-up at Woodward's. His hand somehow got caught in the new-fangled conveyor belt. However, after a quick trip to the hospital and some minor treatment, the hand was deemed OK, as opening day celebrations continued.

"The opening was exciting," recalls Amy Jennings, daughter-in-law of Chinook founder Reg Jennings. "It felt very 'big city.' People from right across the

THEN . . .

Above: Calgarians flocked to Chinook Centre's opening to check out such stores as Woodward's, Holt Renfrew, Spence's and Birks. *Photo courtesy Roy & Amy Jennings*
Below: A mall entrance leading to the Bay is now located close to where the main concourse (pictured above) once stood. *Monica Zurowski photo*

. . . AND NOW

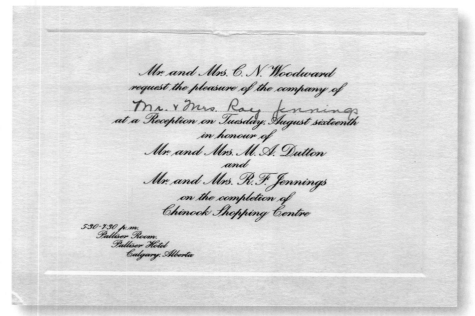

An invitation to a party at the Palliser celebrating Chinook's opening was the hottest ticket in town.

The mall was praised for being "bold (and) forward-looking" by Calgary Mayor Harry Hays, speaking here at the opening ceremony.
Photo courtesy Roy & Amy Jennings

city wanted to be there. The stores were very nice; there were Holt Renfrew and Birks, just to name two."

"Chinook gave people more of a sense of freedom," she says. "There were now shopping options in Calgary. There was more than one place to go when you wanted to shop. And, when you went to Chinook, you weren't dealing with downtown traffic."

On opening day, thousands of Calgarians took in the spectacle of the new Chinook Shopping Centre. Final cost had come in at $12.5 million — $8 million for the buildings and $4 million-plus for the fixtures.

The centre was an open-air mall (except for an underground concourse) and consisted of two sizable blocks of retail stores, along with the substantial Woodward's complex.

Malls of the 1960s were very different from the malls of today. Individuality was encouraged and Chinook Centre was no exception. An initial promotional brochure from the centre's owners encouraged uniqueness. "The services of the developers' architects are available to Chinook Centre tenants for the design and planning of individual stores, to ensure custom planning to suit the individual requirements of each tenant."

As the countdown to the opening ceremonies began, the mall's 3,500 parking stalls filled. Thousands of other Calgarians, anxious to see the shopping centre, created chaos within the public transit system. "Crowds flocking to the opening of the new Chinook Centre caused the Calgary Transit System 'quite a bit of trouble,'" a CTS spokesman told the press.

Woodward's became the favourite shopping choice for many Calgarians, largely because of its quality goods and Food Floor.

Calgary Herald Archive

The regular Manchester morning service, with buses arriving at stops every 20 minutes, became inadequate by 9 a.m. Extra buses were deployed to boost service to every 10 minutes, but the system was still overloaded. Thus, the afternoon service was doubled so that buses were arriving at stops every 7.5 minutes instead of 15 minutes. "That still wasn't enough to handle the crowd," said the CTS. Up to 20 people were waiting at key stops and to some riders' shock, some buses were so full they drove by the stops without pausing for new passengers.

However, those who made it to the mall were treated to the pomp and ceremony befitting such an occasion. Participating in the ceremony were Chunky Woodward, Chinook Shopping Centre president Mervyn (Red) Dutton, vice-president Reg Jennings and general manager Frank Kershaw.

Woodward fired a flare pistol, signalling the natural gas pylon atop the centre's sign to be lit. The Honorable F.C. Colborne, representing the province, congratulated the owners of Chinook and noted that the centre would add to the buoyancy of the economy and provide enjoyment for many Calgarians. "This marks a milestone in the development of the city," Colborne said.

David Sair, president of the Chinook Merchants' Association, presented a large gold key to Calgary Mayor Harry Hays. Hays praised the "bold, forward-looking" centre and hailed the day as the opening of "a new era in shopping" for Calgary citizens.

Hays used the key to open a symbolic large lock, which resulted in ropes and barricades around the centre being removed. Calgarians were admitted to the completed shopping centre for the first time and discovered a world of shopping wonder, exploring stores and services that many described as "very modern."

At Sterling Shoes, for example, 15,000 pairs were for sale in the relatively new "salon style" store. That meant only one pair of each style of shoes was put on display, removing rows of shoeboxes from the shopper's view. If a customer wanted a certain size, the salesperson went to a back room to fetch them.

Chinook Centre's opening day supplement highlighted its unique features, such as a library branch where smoking was allowed (top left.)   Calgary Herald Archive

It was very innovative at the time, as was Sterling's pioneer work in dyeing shoes. "Women's shoes are tinted right on the premises to match anything from hair to handbags and fast service is assured," the store promised in a 40-page advertising supplement published to promote Chinook's grand opening. And, "if you fancy a baby alligator handbag, there's one here for about $300."

Most clothing and accessories, however, were priced in the mid-range. Wool suits for men started at $39.95 at MacLeod Bros. For women, nylons were 39 cents a pair at Reitman's, blouses cost $2.88 to $3.88 at Career Girl and car coats started at $15.88, with prices rising higher if the coats featured the seasonally stylish mink trim.

Betty Shop, which was becoming a favourite stop for women's attire, advertised clothes for the college crowd and beyond. "Women no longer don a black dress and shawl when they hit the 40-year milestone," the shop noted in the opening day supplement. "In many cases it's difficult to tell where the campus years end and the matronly ones begin. Women are dressing gay and young as they please now, ignoring the calendar."

In addition to clothing stores, Chinook Centre housed a florist, bakery, jeweller, furniture shop, drug store, shoe repair, deli, piano store, cigar shop, camera and stationery stop, bowling alley and a Calgary Herald newspaper office. Shoppers could even find a myna bird named

Mickey that greeted visitors at Spence's Shoe Shop.

Sales were featured in every store on opening day. English bone china cups and saucers were $1.50 each, or four for $5, at Birks. McArthur Furniture was selling portable RCA radios for $29.95. At Kresge's, Turkish towels were 59 cents. A .303 calibre sporting rifle was on sale for $23.95 at Finney-Rogers Sports and Hobbies. And, at Penley Drug Store, a little-dab-will-do-you Brylcreem was going for 59 cents.

In addition to 45 stores and services, Chinook was home to a variety of medical offices, belonging to doctors, dentists, chiropractors, X-ray technicians and optometrists. Most of the offices were located in the underground concourse

When Chinook Centre's landmark 24-metre tower, with a gas flame, was installed in 1960, it was the tallest free-standing sign in the city.

Calgary Herald Archive

ANATOMY OF A MALL

- Almost 900 kilometres of reinforced steel were used in construction.
- The plate glass in the centre was enough to provide 12,600 homes with picture windows.
- 4,300 concrete truckloads were required to haul the necessary cement for the centre.
- The electrical conduit pipe used in construction was 87 kilometres, enough to stretch from Chinook to the town of Nanton.
- Chinook's 45 stores would use as much electricity in one day as the average home would use in 20 years.

and were "decorated to achieve an atmosphere of quiet, relaxed optimism," Chinook Centre officials said.

The centre was particularly proud that Dr. Harold R. Antiff opened a bio-clinical laboratory there to specialize in pathological biochemistry. He could complete "thyroid analyses for protein-bound iodine," and perform many hormone tests that were previously done in Regina or Los Angeles.

New ideas and inventions were touted at every turn of the mall. At Woodward's, there were leading-edge cash registers "that do everything but talk," with automatically closing drawers. At the drycleaners, clothing was treated to "the most modern dry-cleaning and shirt service equipment available today." Norman's Beauty Salon not only promised to work magic with your hair; it also boasted a magical "vacuum" floor with special openings that sucked away hair clippings. (In addition, of the 16 salon operators, "at least five of these will be men," the shop promised.)

Even the constant background music filling the centre was a technologi-

THEN . . .

. . . AND NOW

Bentley

Above: This photo of Finney Rogers Sports & Hobbies, taken when the mall opened, conveys a sense of what retail stores looked like in 1960.
Photo courtesy Roy Jennings
Right: Today, the Bentley store makes its home in roughly the same location where Finney Rogers once operated.
Monica Zurowski photo

cal wonder. The music originated at a transmitter in the Greyhound Building downtown, where tape recordings were played. From there, a private telephone line carried the music to Chinook, with a master amplifier in the administration office and speakers situated throughout the mall. The music itself was taped in New York, where industrial psychologists selected the orchestrations.

"It's not just a matter of playing records," the mall noted at the time. "Certain tones that are annoying in certain frequencies are eliminated altogether or modulated to the extent they lose most of their aggravating quality. Tempo is varied and no one instrument, especially horns or woodwinds, is allowed to dominate."

The advertising supplement also reflected many signs of the time, noting one advertiser had been excluded from the publication — the Alberta Government Liquor Store.

"It has been omitted from this supplement because all this Centre literature is advertising and the law states liquor stores shall not advertise," the publication stated.

Another article said the public library branch that was opening in the lower level of the centre would allow smoking: "Good lighting and air-conditioning add extra comfort and make it possible to feature a smoking and browsing room — something new for Calgary."

Above: Last-minute construction occurs at the Chinook Bowladrome, on Aug. 2, 1960.
Right: A group of men ensure the bowling alley is sparkling clean for opening day.
  E.W. Cadman, Oliver Studios; courtesy Bowladrome

MEMORABLE MOMENTS

Ken Penley, owner of Penley Drugs:
"Chinook Centre was popular right from day one," says Penley. He and his wife Prue, both pharmacists, spent the early hours of opening day getting their business ready for the expected shoppers. But as they tried to leave the store to attend the centre's opening ceremonies, a crowd began clamouring to get inside. "We were pushed right back in by customers. . . . People were excited. And, there were a lot of good sales. People wanted to start shopping."

Kip Woodward, whose family owned Woodward's department stores:
"Chinook was a great location for Woodward's," says Kip Woodward, who worked at the Chinook store in the 1970s. "The great thing about Chinook is that at the time it was opening, in the 1960s, Calgary was just getting its legs underneath itself as a city. The growth was remarkable."

One of the most popular places in the mall became the Chinook Bowladrome. With its 32 lanes, it was one of the country's largest bowling alleys at a time when the sport was hitting peak popularity. The facility featured automatic pin setters and "tel-e-scores" which projected bowlers' handwritten scoring sheets onto screens hanging from the ceiling. Also of note were the fibreglass settees, designed in the colours of tangerine and charcoal for the first time in a Canadian bowling facility.

"The Bowladrome quickly became popular with families," says current owner and general manager Fran Clarke. "I think bowling is an activity anyone can do. You don't have to be overly strong. It's a skill that can be easily developed."

As Ralph Klein notes, "Eventually, everyone seemed to go there (the Bowladrome) at one time or another." Klein, a former Calgary mayor and Alberta premier, even belonged to a bowling team there years ago.

Chinook's opening seemed to impact a myriad of aspects of Calgary life. The Calgary Post Office announced that the construction of Chinook made it necessary to add another postal carrier to its staff to take care of this area. The arts and cultural community was intrigued by the opening show of Portuguese artists at the Chinook Art Gallery. And, the pedestrian-friendly aspect of the mall was alluring for those who loved walking or people watching.

"The malls at Chinook Centre are heaven for jaywalkers," said one story in the ad supplement. "No policeman will blow his whistle on you when you cross the street kitty-corner, dawdle in the intersection or stop to chat with friends in the middle of the thoroughfare. Pedestrians and automobiles just don't fraternize here at all. It's a pedestrian paradise."

"Chinook Shopping Centre is a city within a city," the supplement said. "About 1,000 persons are employed within its boundaries, with 1,800 on special sale days. Whether he's a super busy executive or a bus boy, his job is important and affects the smooth working of the entire centre."

THEN ...

Canada's top bowlers gave demos on opening day.
E.W. Cadman, Oliver Studios; courtesy Bowladrome

Progress, however, never stands still. And while Calgarians celebrated the opening of Chinook, the owners were already thinking about future development. The centre's opening day press release noted that an expansion was planned for Chinook. It would include construction of two-storey retail areas that would be enclosed. Other development would feature an eight-storey structure, which would house more stores, a medical clinic and offices. A theatre was being planned, and also being considered were an auditorium and skating rink. The tentative cost would be $4 million to $5 million.

Chinook Centre was indeed becoming a city within a city — a city that was destined to keep growing.

... AND NOW

Calgary Flames player Jarome Iginla hits the lanes
for charity. *Calgary Herald Archive*

CHINOOK CENTRE

SEPT. 28, 1963
Sod is turned for Southridge, a new shopping centre at 4A Street and 59th Avenue S.W.

APRIL 24, 1964
Chinook announces it will soon start a $4 million expansion, including 30 new stores, a theatre and a professional building.

MAY 6, 1965
Stage one of Chinook Centre expansion is completed, with three additional stages slated to open in the next eight months.

OCT. 14, 1965
Southridge Mall opens just north of Chinook, featuring a Simpsons-Sears store, Loblaws and 33 other tenants.

MARCH 17, 1966
Chinook Centre holds first Charity Bazaar, which grows to become an annual, and notable, fundraising event in the city.

SEPT. 30, 1969
Owners of Southridge Mall begin making a play to gain control and ownership of Chinook Centre.

CALGARY & AREA

AUG. 15, 1960
McMahon Football Stadium opens; first game attracts 20,450 fans.

SEPT. 19, 1960
The City of Calgary announces plans for a 270-acre zoo.

JAN. 15, 1961
The jet age arrives in Calgary, as Trans-Canada Airlines (the forerunner of Air Canada) starts a DC-8 jet service to the city.

JULY 9, 1962
The Calgary Stampede turns 50.

1964
Calgary fully annexes the satellite towns of Montgomery and Bowness, a process started a few years earlier.

JULY 1, 1964
Heritage Park, a living historical village, opens.

MARCH 20, 1965
Peter Lougheed (below right) elected leader of Alberta's Progressive Conservative party at age 36.

APRIL 15, 1966
Alberta approves bill that gives the University of Calgary autonomy.

JUNE 10, 1966
Foothills Hospital opens.

FEB. 22, 1967
A $21-million urban renewal scheme for downtown is unveiled, resulting in the eventual razing of scores of historic buildings.

JUNE 30, 1968
The Husky Tower (now the Calgary Tower) opens.

Canwest Archive,
Calgary Herald Archive,
and Chinook Centre Archive

1960s

One word best describes the Sixties — change. It permeated every aspect of life in North America, from politics and the workplace to culture and clothing. Roles were being reversed, rules were being questioned and society was shifting.

The world was rocked by events such as the construction of the Berlin Wall, man's first walk on the moon, political assassinations in the United States, and the arrival of the hippie subculture.

The 1960s saw Canada introduced to social insurance cards, two official languages, the Canada Pension Plan, Expo '67 and Pierre Elliott Trudeau. In Calgary, change was noticeable at almost every street corner.

"It is. . . . a city which is growing fast with a skyline so constantly changing that it would be almost unrecognizable to someone returning after 10 years," the Calgary Herald said in 1964.

During the 1960s, sod was turned for many projects that are still landmarks in the city today — the Foothills Hospital, the Calgary Zoo, Lake Bonavista, the Planetarium (now the Science Centre) and the Calgary Tower, then known as the Husky Tower.

CALGARY'S GROWTH IN THE 1960s

	1959	1969
• Land prices per square foot, near downtown		
	$600	$1,800
• Cost of a single family home		
	$14,000	$22,500
• Land and building assessments		
	$355 million*	$811 million
•Building permits		
	$69 million*	$173 million
• Number of industrial plants		
	388	690
• Wages paid to workers		
	$51 million	$100 million
• Factory shipments		
	$274 million	$500 million

* Figure is from 1960

THEN . . .

The opening of Heritage Park in the 1960s gave Calgarians an ideal place to celebrate the region's roots and history. *Calgary Herald Archive*

This 2009 shot of Heritage Park shows the same building that is featured in the photo above, but also depicts how the park and its vegetation have matured. *Grant Black photo*

. . . AND NOW

Several of these local landmark projects involved Chinook Centre's principals. Red Dutton, who never met a challenge he could ignore, agreed to build the 19,000-seat McMahon Stadium in 100 days. George McMahon, financing the stadium's construction, didn't believe the job could be completed that quickly, so he bet Dutton $1,000 that the deadline would be missed. Dutton completed the project three days early. McMahon, of course, paid off the bet — all in pennies.

Heritage Park was another project in Calgary near to the heart of Chinook founders, particularly Reg Jennings. Much of the park's land was donated, thanks to Jennings. His construction firm provided a foreman to oversee the building of the facility. Even today, his son, daughter-in-law and grandchildren are vital volunteers, fundraisers and donors at the park.

The 1960s not only saw new landmarks sprouting up in Calgary. The city also experienced expansion in its arts and educational scenes. Theatre Calgary and the Calgary Philharmonic performed regularly. The Alberta College of Art opened; Mount Royal College became a public institution; SAIT grew its technologies and applied arts programs; and, the University of Calgary gained autonomy from the University of Alberta.

Changes in the workplace occurred, too, as women questioned their roles in society and the workforce. In 1961, 8.4 per cent of Alberta women who worked outside the home were employed as "salesclerks," according to government statistics. By 1971, that number had dropped to 6.1 per cent, as females explored a greater variety of career choices.

The city continued to grow. At the end of 1961, Calgary doubled its size in area from 74 to 150 square miles. This annexation included Forest Lawn; a parcel of adjoining industrial land on the eastern outskirts of the city; a three-mile strip of land to the south of the city; and, parts of Montgomery and Bowness. (Both communities were fully annexed within two years.)

MEMORABLE MOMENTS

Grant Black photo

Calgary Herald Archive

Al Hardstaff, Chinook merchant for 47 years and former owner of Chinook Optical:
"I remember the first manager, Ken McGregor, burning rubber in the parking lot, in his '63 teal green Pontiac, and trying to chase merchants and employees out of the prime parking spots early in the morning. Merchant parking has been a pain in the butt for Chinook since day one."

Phil Brien, Chinook customer:
As a Milton Williams Junior High student in the 1970s, Brien would head to Chinook after classes. "My brother and I, and (two) friends, would spend our pocket change on buying fresh mini-donuts from Woodward's. The sugary treats were a great source of fun and amusement to watch being cooked and twirled through the hot oil merry-go-round . . . Sorry to have seen Milton Williams School, Woodward's and the donuts pass on in history, but (they're) still retained in Chinook lore."

Jon Love, KingSett Capital:
"My father, Don Love, founded Oxford in Edmonton in 1960. The acquisition of the properties that would eventually combine to become Chinook was part of the company's early expansion and the first of many to create a super regional mall. It was a very successful project, both financially and aesthetically, and began the legacy of what Chinook is today."

Lee Richardson, Member of Parliament for Calgary Centre (Chinook is in his constituency):
Richardson recalls Chinook was the No. 1 spot for part-time work, so he applied at Woodward's ski shop, where Susie (his future wife) was working. "They were desperate for an expert skier to complement the less experienced staff," he says. "Well, I could hardly get down the hill in those days and didn't know the difference between my old wooden skis and the fancy new 'metallics' that had just arrived, but I gave personnel a good story. They didn't even check my resume. I started my new part-time job the same day." Years later, Richardson was a volunteer with the then-relatively-unknown Peter Lougheed. They headed to Chinook to do some handshaking. Most people ignored Lougheed until CFCN TV dropped by to "film this new campaign method of 'meeting the people.' The bright lights and TV camera attracted attention. From that day on, our young Chinook team always brought a small TV camera and big lights. No one in the large crowds that gathered around and jostled to 'get in the shot' with the future premier suspected that it was a rented camera with no film in it."

Jackie Long, Chinook customer:
"My mom, my cousin and three of my sisters took the long bus ride (from Bowness) out to the grand reopening (when Chinook and Southridge joined together). . . . When we finished walking around we were all so tired. My mom decided to pick up a few things at the Safeway and that is when she noticed the promotion that du Maurier cigarettes had. They were giving away free cigarettes and offering rides home. We were all quite surprised and happy when the driver agreed to take us all out to Bowness and my mom even got a free package of cigarettes. Lucky for us, he had a station wagon."

THEN . . .

. . . AND NOW

When Chinook Centre opened, it was on the city's outskirts, as was the Foothills Hospital, pictured above while under construction in 1962.
Over the decades, the hospital has continued to grow, as seen in the photo at the right.

Calgary Herald Archive photos

CANADIAN IDOL, CIRCA 1965

• A promotion aimed at teens and young adults caused a frenzy in 1965 when plans were revealed that Bobby Curtola, "the Ontario idol of Canada's younger set," would be featured at Woodward's Salute to Youth Show, Aug. 19 to 21.

• Thirteen girls, who'd been selected as Woodward's Fashionettes 1965-66, would model twice each night and audience members would vote to determine which girl should become Miss Fashionette.

• Miss Fashionette would win a dinner date with Bobby Curtola.

• The youth show also gave local groups a chance to display promotional material at the mall, which included booths from 4-H clubs, Junior Achievement, YMCA, YWCA, Girl Guides, Brownies, Boy Scouts and Air Cadets.

the continent and Chinook Centre often hosted bands in centre court.

"It was a totally different time in our lives," says media personality Don Wood, who hosted Teen and Twenty Dance Parties for CFCN. "Calgary was a close-knit community" and that was especially evident at the Chinook Stampede Breakfast, says Wood, who would broadcast live from the event. "I don't think there is any kind of community feeling that could match those breakfasts."

"Chinook was where it was at," adds long-time Chinook merchant Don McGregor. "This was the place to come. This was the place to be seen. When rock and roll came along, Chinook jumped on it and invited the community to see bands at the shopping centre."

"Overall. . . . it seemed almost right from the start that the community of Calgary took pride and delight in this place," he says.

One of the key areas that delighted Calgarians continued to be Woodward's. It was a significant draw with its Food Floor, "$1.49 day" sales and a top-notch restaurant with features such as a toasted shrimp salad sandwich.

When people visited the shopping centre, they usually said they were going to Woodward's as opposed to Chinook Centre, notes Sheldon Streifel, co-owner of the Chinook Barber Shop.

"They called the entire place Woodward's, not Chinook. . . . that's how big Woodward's was," says Streifel.

Customers and staff were always made to feel welcome at Woodward's, says Do-

CHINOOK CENTRE **CPAir** present

FESTIVAL OF THE ORIENT

港九新界名庭
龍舟競賽盛況
中區兩龍舟撞斷龍西漁業秘冠軍

CPAir

3 BIG DAYS
THURS. FRI. SAT.
Featuring
ORIENTAL• ORIENTAL
DISPLAYS• PRODUCTS
ORIENTAL ENTERTAINMENT
plus

Miss Ng Kim-Sheung   Miss Tin Yin-Yung
DIRECT FROM HONG KONG
CP AIR & HONK KONG TOURIST ASS'N.

FOON YING!
A CHINESE SAYING
WHICH MEANS WELCOME!
the **FOON YING** TO THE
HOUSE of CHINOOK
SEE
• JAPANESE DANCING
• KOREAN DANCING
• KARATE
• JUDO
• CHINESE LION DANCE
• JAPANESE DOLL and KIMONO DISPLAY
• GIANT PAGODA
AND MANY OTHER ATTRACTIONS
Sayonara!

The mall came alive with dance, food and art demonstrations for the Festival of the Orient in the '60s.

Beth Jennings, wife of mall founder Reg Jennings, takes in Old Fashioned Days, a successful promotion that saw merchants and customers dress for the occasion. Photo courtesy Amy & Roy Jennings

From its inception 50 years ago, Chinook Centre's Breakfast became one of the most popular Stampede events in the city during the annual July festivities.
Courtesy Chinook Centre

MEMORABLE MOMENTS

Don Thomas, former CFCN radio program director:

The station held a Stampede beard-growing contest and needed a place to host the judging, so Chinook Centre agreed to host a breakfast. "We didn't know exactly what to expect. We begged and borrowed all kinds of things. . . . We went home and got about two or three hours of sleep and when we got back about 5:30 a.m., there were people waiting. . . . We had one long table and people walked up, crowding around without a real line-up. After waiting a while, people began to elbow each other a bit. The actual count of how many people were there was 10,000. We ran out of coffee. . . . The pancake house nearby did a great business that day because people got tired of waiting for the free breakfast. . . . The astronomical thing is that the breakfast is still going strong. We weren't looking to establish something that would last a half-century."

reen Morgan, who worked in the store's lingerie department for 20 years. Her Woodward's position was the first job outside the home for the mother of three, who still remembers the close friendships that formed between employees. "It was a wonderful place. It was always fun. . . . especially on special event days."

Mall manager Ken McGregor used his marketing talents to implement those events, unlike anything seen before in the city. Hawaiian Days, Old Fashioned Days and Days of the Orient became annual affairs that attracted thousands.

"They were quite inventive," says Amy Jennings, daughter-in-law of Chinook founder Reg Jennings. Entertainment, for example, would be flown to Calgary from places like Samoa to lend authentic-

ity to Hawaiian Days. Shoppers could enter contests to win trips to exotic locales. Mall merchants would host sales around these events, dress up in costumes and decorate their stores, transforming the mall into some far-away land.

The promotions and contests were unique, says Roger Jarvis, who was a rep for the now-defunct Canadian Pacific Airlines and who worked with the mall on contests such as trip give-aways to Mexico City and Hong Kong.

"It was a good outlet; it was the biggest," says Jarvis. "If you wanted to do something that caught people's attention, Chinook was the place to do it. . . . McGregor would try anything."

One of Chinook's most significant contributions to the community became the

Above: This 1963 sketch shows the elevated, glass-covered Southridge Mall that was to be built just north of Chinook.
Right: Simpsons-Sears, under construction here in 1963, would be the anchor tenant of Southridge.
Calgary Herald Archive

Charity Bazaar. The event started in 1966 to increase awareness of local charities and a wide variety of church groups, while also providing a venue for them to raise funds. The participating groups largely sold non-manufactured and non-professional items, meaning the bazaar was a treasure chest of handicrafts, hand-made items and baked goods.

Chinook's most enduring event, however, continued to be its annual Stampede Breakfast. Almost immediately upon its inception, the breakfast became a "must attend" event each July.

"It was a breakfast on a massive scale," says Roy Warhurst, a musician-producer, who oversaw entertainment for the event for 30-plus years. "We had stacks of talent," he says. "Almost every high profile country musician, we've had at the breakfast."

In Calgary, Chinook winds have become legendary. These are the warm, dry winds that blow down the eastern slopes of the Rockies and dramatically increase the temperature on a winter's day. They represent positive change.

It's fitting, therefore, that Chinook Centre was named after these winds, since the mall quickly became a venue of change, especially for young, ambitious merchants wanting to shake up the retail scene.

The mall provided significant opportunities for entrepreneurs. Don McGregor was one of many young Calgarians entering the world of retail during Chinook's first decade. In 1968, he opened Orange Julius in the mall; he and his father learned about the franchise from the Seattle World's Fair.

Another young mall merchant, J.W.

In September 1963, sod was turned for the $3 million Southridge Mall. Pictured are G.D. Love of Edmonton, president of Oxford Leaseholds, Southridge's owner; Merle Courtright, Calgary manager of Simpsons-Sears; J.W. Button of Toronto, president of Simpsons-Sears, one of the mall's major tenants; Mayor Grant MacEwan; and A.A. Shelly of Calgary, vice-president and general manager of Loblaws, another major tenant.

Calgary Herald Archive

A TALE OF TWO SHOPPING CENTRES

	SOUTHRIDGE	CHINOOK CENTRE
		(including the 1965 expansion)
Size of site:	10 acres	40 acres
Store space:	215,000 square feet	700,000 square feet
Number of stores:	35	70
Parking:	600 to 800 cars	3,000 to 3,500 cars
Anchor store:	Simpsons-Sears	Woodward's
Grocery store:	Loblaws	Woodward's Food Floor

(Boots) Rogers, says there was no better place than Chinook to start a business. On Chinook's opening day, he introduced the city to Finney Rogers Sports & Hobbies, co-owned with hockey player Sid Finney and Roy Jennings.

"Chinook provided an opportunity for local merchants," says Rogers, who'd dreamed of owning a sporting goods store since being a kid. "There were a lot of local businesses and everyone in there knew each other. Everyone was so friendly. Without a doubt, we were like a family."

All the merchants looked out for each other and for the mall, adds optician Al Hardstaff, former owner of Chinook Optical. Hardstaff — who retired in spring 2009, after spending 40-plus years working and owning a business at the mall — credits the Chinook Merchants' Association with making a difference in how things were run.

The businesses displayed a high regard for each other and their landlord, notes Ken Penley of Penley Drugs. "We were treated well by the founders of Chinook, so that respect was shown back to them."

As opposed to the national and international chain stores that now make their homes in shopping centres, Chinook in the 1960s was dominated by local businesses, says Phil Streifel, long-time barber and co-owner of the Chinook Barber Shop.

"There were so many independent merchants," says Streifel. "That made Chinook. Mr. Jennings, Mr. Dutton and the other owners had said that they wanted local tenants. They treated us with respect. . . . They tried to give local small businesses a break."

A visit to the Chinook Barber Shop today still provides an interesting flash of the past. While two of Phil's sons, Sheldon and James, run the shop, Phil — who turned 89 years young in July 2009 — still occasionally cuts hair. Haircuts have gone up a bit in price — from $1.75 in 1960 to $18 today, but GST is included. Phil and his wife Kat continue to be devoted to the business, and even

MEMORABLE MOMENTS

Rt. Hon. Joe Clark, former Prime Minister of Canada:

"When I was a candidate in the 1967 provincial election, in the then-constituency of Calgary South, most of whose residents shopped at Chinook Centre, I thought that would be a fine place to meet them and pass out my propaganda. But (I) was informed, unceremoniously, that political canvassing was not allowed to interfere with the serious business of shopping. . . . I (also) remember the Stampede Breakfasts in the parking area of Chinook, where thousands attended, from literally around the globe, and I regularly demonstrated that my skills were more suited to the House of Commons than they were to flipping flapjacks."

Don McGregor, long-time Chinook businessman:

Shortly after opening his first Orange Julius shop in the mall (an original menu is below), McGregor noticed a problem with the drain near his outlet. "We went to the centre's underground tunnels to check out the situation and found the drain was clogged with organic waste and dirt from the nearby Woodward's pet department," he recalls. As a small group started to clean the pipes, they were surprised by live eels that jumped out of the drain. "It was not what you'd expect to see."

Grant Black photo

Calgary Herald Archive

ORANGE JULIUS MENU

DRINKS		HOT DOGS	
SMALL	15¢	MONGREL	30¢
REGULAR	25¢	(MUSTARD RELISH ONIONS)	
LARGE	35¢	PICKLE POOCH	30¢
JUMBO	55¢	(MUSTARD & PICKLE)	
FAMILY PAK	95¢	CHILI DOG	35¢
(WITH EGG 10¢ EXTRA)		(WITH 2 OZ PORTION OF CHILI)	

"A Devilish Good Drink"

stop by the shop to clean, ensuring everything is in sparkling shipshape.

"I've been a barber for over 68 years," says Phil. "It's been interesting . . . (and) Chinook has been a good place to be."

Chinook Centre, however, wasn't the only mall vying for Calgarians' attention and dollars in the 1960s. The rise of shopping centres was fuelled by the excellent financial results owners were seeing across the continent.

"Shopping centres rank as one of the best forms of investment," A.E. Diamond, the former chairman and co-founder of Cadillac Fairvew, once said.

Now, a new shopping competitor was about to arrive on the scene right next door to Chinook.

In September 1963, Oxford Leaseholds Ltd., of Edmonton, announced plans for a new shopping centre, Southridge, to be constructed just north of Chinook. On a 10-acre site at 59th Avenue and 4A Street Southwest, Oxford said it would build a multimillion-dollar development, featuring an 80,000 square foot Simpsons-Sears department store and a Loblaws grocery store.

While the proposed mall was considerably smaller than the 40-acre Chinook Centre site, Calgarians were intrigued by the new approach to the centre. The designers of Southridge, J.H. Cook and Associates of Calgary, said the facility would feature an elevated glass-enclosed shopping plaza.

"The development is described as a totally new concept in department store design, leading to new techniques in merchandising," newspapers reported.

The plaza would be built above Simpsons-Sears, reached by escalators, and house at least 20 additional shops. In its entirety, the centre would be 120,000 square feet in size and provide parking for 600 to 800 cars. Its opening was scheduled for 1965.

Not to be overshadowed, however, Chinook Centre gave a statement to the press on the same day Southridge was announced. Ken McGregor released de-

Above: Red Dutton watches a crane at work as construction kicks off for the expansion of the Chinook Shopping Centre in September of 1964. Right: Dutton places his hands in cement to officially start the expansion.

Calgary Herald Archive

tails of Chinook's expansion, which he said could include a possible high-rise office or apartment building.

The expansion would involve new retail stores, office space, medical offices and additional recreational facilities. When complete, the mall would include about 600,000 to 700,000 square feet of retail and service space, compared to its 1963 size of 450,000 square feet.

Chinook Centre publicly stated it would welcome the addition of Southridge to the neighbourhood, noting the new mall would increase shop and service offerings to Calgarians, thus increasing the number of shoppers who'd be attracted to the area.

Chinook Centre's first expansion in the mid-1960s created jobs for dozens of people, much as it does during renovations even today.

Calgary Herald Archive

However, friction quickly developed when Oxford proposed relocating 4A Street Southwest about 75 yards west. Oxford said the move would give it additional room that was required to develop the west side of Southridge and ensure it could provide appropriate parking for a major business on that side of the site.

Chinook responded by saying this road change would impact "convenient traffic movement, . . . impair access and egress to Chinook Centre and seriously prejudice its businessmen."

City council began examining the proposal in February, but the strong opposition led to the matter being referred for discussion and study several times. The delays became such that Oxford warned the centre may not be built. "If Calgary does not want this development, we can always move elsewhere," said R.D.S. Reid, a manager for the Oxford group.

He noted the centre would provide 600 jobs, with a $2-million annual payroll, and pay taxes of $150,000. "We are hanging on the ropes right now," Reid said.

A compromise between the two shopping centres was eventually reached after a three-hour city hall meeting. The result was that 4A Street was relocated somewhere in the middle of where each shopping centre wanted it.

As construction on Southridge began, Chinook's growth plan also moved forward. On Sept. 15, 1964, work began on a $3.5-million expansion to Chinook. Dutton oversaw the start of the construction by directing a crane operator to remove a large concrete slab from the existing centre.

The expansion would include an 800-seat "motion pictures theatre" on the top level of the centre, along with a six or seven-storey professional building

Top right: Lynn Jennings, granddaughter of Chinook founder Reg Jennings, and local promotions rep Lois Kimball, present a gold key to open stage two of Chinook's 1965 expansion. Stage two featured the opening of Chinook's movie theatre; the official program is above, courtesy Amy & Roy Jennings. At left is the punch card used to win prizes during stage one of the expansion opening.

OPENING OCT. 14

there's a world of quality at

SOUTHRIDGE Mall

"A NEW CONCEPT IN SHOPPING"

AT MACLEOD TRAIL AND 58TH AVENUE SOUTH WEST

Shown here at Southridge's opening, Oct. 14, 1965, are Bill Dickie, MLA for Calgary-Glenmore; A.A. Shelly, vice-president of Loblaws; G.D. Love, president of Oxford Leaseholds Ltd.; J.C. Barrow, executive vice-president of Simpsons-Sears; and J.W. Button, president of Simpsons-Sears.

Calgary Herald Archive

providing 50,000 square feet of office space, 30 new stores and a liquor outlet.

Importantly, more than $500,000 of the expansion cost would be spent on constructing one giant roof, enclosing the entire mall. "The malls will be air conditioned and have a year-round temperature of 72 degrees," the media reported. "Trees, shrubbery, park-like seats and fountains will provide a garden-like atmosphere." April 1, 1965 was the scheduled opening day.

Meanwhile at the Southridge site, retail space was 90 per cent leased by November 1964. The mall now included 35 shops, with the largest two being Simpsons-Sears Ltd. and Loblaw Grocerterias Company Ltd.

Southridge would be 125,000 square feet in size on the lower level and 86,000 on the upper. Simpsons-Sears was scheduled to occupy the entire lower level (and some of upper), while Loblaws and 33 smaller stores would utilize the upper area.

Even though the two shopping centres were still separate entities, many people were already thinking of them as one. "When completed, Southridge, along with the Chinook Shopping Centre to the immediate south, and Canada Safeway to the north, will form the largest centre complex in Western Canada," the Herald reported.

On May 6, 1965, Chinook Centre unveiled its expansion, five months before Southridge opened its doors. Stores and services now numbered 70. With the expansion, Chinook owners had invested $16 million in capital in the centre. The results were almost 700,000 square feet of development and 2,000 jobs, along with incredible fashion offerings.

"A vision of mammoth development and extreme pride and optimism in their city have paid off in success and satisfaction for a group of Calgary businessmen," said an article in the mall's expansion supplement published in May 1965.

The supplement also noted this May opening was only stage one of Chinook's expansion.

Stage two, featuring the new Chinook

Reflecting popular trends of the 1960s, Woodward's offered a wide array of curling fashions in 1963. In 1969, the still pricey colour television set was the hot item of the day.

Theatre, was scheduled to be finished June 15. Stage three, featuring the complete enclosure of all parts of the centre, would be done on Aug. 10. And, stage four — the Chinook Professional Building — was slated to open Jan. 1, 1966.

This professional tower represented a trend Chinook helped start on its opening day in 1960 — the tendency of some medical and dental offices to leave the downtown core.

Prior to the 1960s, a visit to the doctor or dentist generally meant a trip downtown. But a few trailblazing medical professionals began setting up offices outside the city centre, including some in Chinook's lower mall in 1960.

"It was quite an innovation to move out of the core," says optometrist Dr. Bernie Tharp, who launched his Chinook practice when the centre opened.

Patients liked the concept. Parking was convenient and they could easily do other errands while at Chinook. Medical professionals enjoyed it, too.

"There was very much a community feel there," says Tharp. "Everybody knew everybody."

When the professional tower opened in 1966, Tharp moved his practice from the lower mall to the tower and turned the lower mall space into Chinook Optical. He eventually sold that business to Al Hardstaff, who lovingly grew the business, moved it upstairs, and sold it in recent years as he prepared for retirement. The buyer? Tharp's daughter, Biba.

"It's gone full circle," says Tharp.

Southridge opened Oct. 14, 1965, touting the message that the centre represented

Jean Leslie, married to Jack Leslie, Calgary mayor from 1965 to 1969:
"Woodward's was a favourite store for us, and for many other Calgarians. . . . They outfitted Jack with a jacket for a Grey Cup parade. They always had quality merchandise."

Photo courtesy Laureen Harper

Calgary Herald Archive

Laureen Harper, wife of Prime Minister Stephen Harper:
"When I was a little girl my parents always took us from Turner Valley to Calgary to look at the Christmas lights. We always finished off with a visit to Santa at Chinook Centre (as pictured above.) I remember giant candy canes lit up on the side of the Sears store. But my fondest memory was the year they had a bunch of telephones set up, so that you could listen to Santa and the elves. We didn't have a phone at home at that time, so being able to listen to the North Pole conversations was a particular thrill."

shopping in its finest environment. "The most advanced concept in design of major shopping centres has been incorporated in the Southridge Mall," said an article in the centre's opening day advertising supplement. "(It) has been developed as a modern, all-weather, family shopping plaza."

Highlights of the mall included a Pennington's clothing store for "forgotten" women; the Alpine Hut ski store; a delicatessen featuring barbecue chicken, roast and sausage; and shops selling everything from flowers and fabrics to linens and leather.

The anchor department store, Simpsons-Sears, was the second in the city and promised all modern conveniences for shoppers, including a distinctive millinery and elegant salon. "Scientific planning ensures customer convenience,"

the store said, which resulted in displays that saw shirts grouped together by sizes and handbags sorted by colours.

The increased variety of stores brought a fashion windfall to the city. Styles of the Sixties were readily available at Chinook and Southridge. Gone were the poodle skirts and cat-eye glasses of the 1950s. Taking their place were wire-framed glasses and the miniskirt, first popularized by Mary Quant in Britain.

At the same time, nothing said sophistication like a pastel suit, with a short, boxy jacket and matching pillbox hat, thanks to style icon and U.S. first lady Jacqueline Kennedy. At the same time, more men began going without hats, thanks to her husband, John F. Kennedy — the first U.S. president who didn't regularly wear a chapeau. Another significant fashion trend for men was that

ties got wider — up to five inches at times.

For women, almost anything seemed to go. Pants became acceptable for most occasions. Women said hello to gauchos, fishnet stockings, medallions, belts, knit fabrics and polyester. Hot pants, bell-bottoms and skinny jeans were introduced. Capris, tent dresses, peasant blouses, caftans, tie-dyed materials and paisleys proved popular. Footwear included platform shoes, stilettos and white go-go boots, while make-up trends featured blue and green eye shadows, false eyelashes and pale lipstick.

Women's hairdos ranged from the beehive to the long and straight, while men began growing longer hair, sideburns, moustaches and beards.

Importantly, women threw their nylons away and welcomed pantyhose, one

1960s
ON THE CATWALK

Bold and bright
or short and swinging,
fashion in the '60s
reflected changing times.

Chinook Centre began hosting fashion shows right from its opening, to provide Calgarians with a look at the hottest styles of the day.
Kenny Galleries photos; courtesy Patti Falconer Agency

of the Chinook Centre's most popular items in the 1960s.

The Chinook expansion and Southridge opening, however, impacted more than the city's style. A growing number of stores and services wanted to be near the boom occurring around the malls and take advantage of the area's traffic.

A thriving community of businesses developed in the area, says Shelley McCullough, president and owner of Maclin Ford. "Chinook Centre produced many customers for us, just as we produced customers for them. . . . When people were waiting for their cars, they'd often go over to Chinook," she says. The traffic headed to Chinook also produced great exposure for neighbouring businesses like Maclin (now relocated in the Calgary Auto Mall.)

Over the years, Macleod Trail became quite a busy route, says Larry Ryder, whose family owned the Trade Winds Hotel across the street from Chinook.

"It was a good place to do business," he says, noting Chinook was one of the reasons that the Trade Winds was built where it was.

Chinook's success and the emergence of other malls in the city were also impacting Calgary's downtown. This led to an urban renewal program focused on rebuilding the city centre into the major shopping area.

"It is our plan to maintain a strong downtown core without harming the neighbourhood shopping centres," Ald. Jack Davis said at the time.

It was no surprise people were paying attention to Chinook and its impacts on the city. There were similar scenes playing out across the continent.

"Developers have made brilliant use of shopping centres to dominate the new retail space market in Canadian cities since 1950," said James Lorimer, in his book The Developers. "The success of shopping centres has produced a host of important changes in the structure of cities, in the retailing business, in the position of independent small business-men versus the national retail chains, and in the choices people encounter as shoppers," he notes.

People were becoming accustomed to driving to a mall to shop, as opposed to walking through a downtown district. Stores were no longer street-front enti-ties, but blocked off in privately owned malls, Lorimer said. Shop owners were no longer property owners, but mer-chants who paid rent. Malls were de-pendent on large retail chains, and often grocery stores, for success, he said.

"Shopping centres did much more than provide the kind of local shop-ping facilities traditional for shopping districts. They also attracted the kind of retail business that had previously gone downtown, and substantially weakened the dominance of downtown businesses over their local markets," said Lorimer.

Despite all the change that occurred in the 1960s, there was one last monumen-tal shift in store for Chinook before the decade ended.

As 1969 drew to a close, news broke that the owners of Southridge were making a play for control of Chinook. Oxlea In-vestments Ltd. — a member of the Ed-monton-based Oxford Leasehold Ltd. group — began making a bid to obtain a controlling interest in Chinook. The shopping centre issued a news release that Oxlea had taken options from cer-tain individual Chinook shareholders to acquire holdings.

"If the options were exercised, Oxlea planned within a period of two years to make an offer to acquire all of the com-mon shares of Chinook," the Herald re-ported Oct. 1, 1969. Chinook Centre was again on a track of transformation.

Chinook's annual reports show, from top to bottom, an artist's rendering of the professional tower in 1964, the crowds at the mall's special events, including Hawaiian Days in 1966, and an aerial shot of the mall in 1967.

CHINOOK CENTRE

JAN. 29, 1970
The sale of Chinook Centre to Oxford, the owners of Southridge Mall, is announced.

MAY 10, 1971
Chinook and Southridge publicly announce plans to combine into one shopping centre, to be called Chinook-Ridge Centre.

JULY 18, 1972
Chinook-Ridge applies for a city permit to link the two mall structures and close the street between them.

APRIL 24, 1973
Chinook-Ridge says it will keep a drive-through road open between the two malls, but it will build a bridge over that road, while also expanding retail and parking space.

MAY 15, 1974
Mall owners announce the two merged shopping centres will be known as Chinook Centre, as opposed to Chinook-Ridge. The next day, Chinook Centre officially unveils its latest expansion, which sees the two formerly separate malls connected by a second-level bridge.

CALGARY & AREA

AUGUST 1970
Calgary's first public housing project, Baker House, opens its doors.

DEC. 30, 1970
New home prices drop slightly from the 1969 highs, which averaged $15,900 to $22,500.

AUG. 30, 1971
Peter Lougheed and his Conservative Party win the provincial election and end 36 years of Social Credit rule in Alberta.

SEPT. 11, 1972
City hall gives approval to close 60th Avenue between the two malls.

OCT. 15, 1973
Calgary's economy booms due to the Arab oil embargo.

JUNE 23, 1974
The $14-million grandstand and racetrack hold an open house for their new operations at Stampede Park.

NOV. 15, 1974
Prime Minister John Diefenbaker opens the Calgary Convention Centre.

MAY 8, 1975
The last trolley buses make their final run in Calgary.

SEPT. 22, 1976
The Glenbow-Alberta Institute (now the Glenbow Museum) is opened.

SEPT. 1, 1977
Alberta highway signs are converted to metric.

OCT. 12, 1977
Phase one of the Calgary International Airport is completed.

AUG. 16, 1978
The city, now with a population over 500,000, celebrates the opening of Sikome Lake; Fish Creek Park becomes one of the country's largest provincial parks within an urban setting.

1970s

Seize the opportunity. The philosophy worked for dozens of entrepreneurs who set up shop in Chinook Centre over the years. They followed their own paths, opened themselves to innovation and, importantly, never flinched at a hard day's work.

As a result, Chinook became a hub of local business activity in the 1960s — a trend that continued to blossom in the '70s. Impressively selling everything from soup to nuts and haircuts to hockey jerseys, entrepreneurs ran their businesses with affection and attention.

Calgarians loved the mall and the mall loved Calgary. As co-founder Mervyn (Red) Dutton noted in one of the early company reports, "Public acceptance of the centre continues to be highly gratifying."

That acceptance is a sentiment many long-time Calgarians remember. "You could get everything you wanted there," says Rod Sykes, Calgary mayor from 1969 to 1977. "It was not only the shops and staff that made you want to go there. Chinook was connected to the community, too," he notes, recalling that managers of the Woodward's and Sears stores, for example, were members of local Rotary clubs.

"There were so many local retailers there who had a tremendous sense of pride in Chinook, in their community and in their businesses," says Bob Knight, who became the shopping centre's marketing director in 1977. "All these local businesses combined to provide a shopping experience at Chinook that was different from anywhere else.

THE 1970s: YOU CAN SHOP UNTIL YOU DROP

• In 1956 there were 64 shopping centres in the country; by 1973 there were 644, according to Statistics Canada.
• In 1956, retail sales in shopping centres totalled $233 million, representing 1.8 per cent of all retail spending. In 1973, that same sales figure ballooned to $6.7 billion and represented 17 per cent of all retail sales dollars.
• Construction of regional shopping centres (built to serve larger areas than traditional malls) exploded during the 1960s. While only 15 existed in Canada in 1959, that number grew to 101 by 1973.

The Forzani brothers – John, left, Tom, centre, and Joe – all played for the Calgary Stampeders in the 1970s, while dreaming up a business plan to open a chain of sporting goods stores. Calgary Herald Archive

"I learned so much; there were so many great people who worked there — people who lived and breathed service and quality," says Knight. "I felt like I was at the University of Shopping Centres. It changed me professionally and I think it changed me as a human being, too."

A community feeling definitely permeated the shopping centre, adds Ron Renaud, mall manager in the late 1970s and now president of Rencor Developments. "It was a friendly centre in a friendly city. The people really made that place."

"From the ownership to the tenants to customers, everyone had good relationships," says Carmine D'Ambola, who ran the Esquire Barber Shop in the mall for about a quarter century.

"The owners, Mr. Dutton and Mr. Jennings, treated us quite well. It was a very good place to run a small business," adds D'Ambola, who still sees many of his Chinook regulars at his current downtown barber shop.

Many merchants, past and current, believe Chinook was a defining factor in the success of numerous local businesses. For those stores that prospered in Chinook, the experience seemed almost magical.

"When you first start out with a small business, it's feast or famine," says John Forzani, co-founder of the Forzani Group and co-owner of the Calgary Stampeders. "You wonder how you're going to make it from payroll to payroll at times."

Forzani was still playing football with the

The 1970s were a time of growth and prosperity in Calgary, which was good for the city and good for retailers at Chinook Centre, says Morley Sklar.
Grant Black photo

Stamps when he opened his first store (Forzani's Locker Room) in 1974 with brothers Joe and Tom, and friend Basil Bark. Three years later they bought the Finney Rogers sporting goods store in Chinook, turning it into a third Forzani's location.

"I thought if we could get 10 or 15 stores in Southern Alberta, it would be great," says Forzani. "I didn't imagine what it would grow to become." The Forzani Group evolved into Canada's biggest, and only, national sporting goods retailer with more than 464 corporate and franchise stores. The group's stores include retail outlets such as Sport Mart, Sport Chek, Athletes World and Coast Mountain Sports. Annual sales top the $1-billion mark.

"We got in the right industry at the right time," says Forzani. Jogging, fitness and team sports exploded in popularity in the 1970s and everyone needed athletic footwear. But the early days of the business, especially before opening in Chinook, were challenging.

The Chinook location opened at the start of December, the busiest month of the year for retailers. Team jerseys for the Stampeders and the Calgary Cowboys hockey team were the popular sellers.

"In our free-standing stores, we'd sell five, maybe 10, jerseys a day," recalls Forzani. "In Chinook, I'd bring in 100 at a time . . . and they'd be gone — fast. We did so much more business that very first month. We couldn't believe it made such a big difference — selling the same product at the same price point — but selling it in the mall. . . . We did one

ODDS AND ENDS AT CHINOOK IN THE 1970s

• Police were puzzled over the discovery of two sticks of high quality dynamite found in a women's washroom in the Simpson-Sears store. The sticks weren't attached to a detonating device, but police closed the store for 45 minutes. The dynamite was later detonated at the Sarcee military reserve.
• Theatre Calgary publicity director Ron Rosvold lived in a tree house, atop a 30-foot scaffold outside the entrance of Chinook Centre for a week. He dropped theatre brochures to people, in a bid to sell 5,000 subscriptions. Food and water were delivered with a pulley system.
• In 1974, Thrifty's ran a unique promotion, in which they displayed a huge pair of pants, with a 76-inch waist and 45-inch length. If anyone of Goliath-sized proportions found the pants fit him, he could keep them free of charge. The pants went unclaimed.

Jim Dinning, long-time MLA and former Provincial Treasurer:
Every year, Woodward's organized a fashion council, consisting of a male and female student from each Calgary high school. Dinning, who graduated from Western Canada High in 1970, was one of his school's representatives on the council, an impressive appointment among city teens. "We would do the occasional fashion show. . . . and we worked at Woodward's. I was selling sweaters and pants and socks and men's underwear. I made $2 an hour. I remember jumping for joy when my boss told me I was getting a raise to $2.10. It was a great high school job."

Doreen Morgan, long-time Woodward's employee:
"The sales for $1.49 days (at Woodward's) were remarkable. . . . You'd always know when it had been a $1.49 day because the next day, you'd see kids walking by, on their way to school, in new T-shirts and runners."

Jack Donahue, well-known local lawyer:
As a young man, Donahue worked in Woodward's at Chinook, while on breaks from university. "Wooward's was very different for Calgary at the time. . . . Its Food Floor was the first place that I ever saw a live lobster," Donahue recalls. "Chinook Centre grew and it became a place that all Calgarians look at as their shopping centre."

Din Peerani, owner of Formans Fashion Group:
"As retailers, we looked out for each other and treated each other well. There were a few menswear shops in the mall in the '70s. If we couldn't help a customer and we didn't have what he wanted, we'd refer him to one of our competitors who possibly had the stock. Customers appreciated that. They knew they could trust us. . . . the customers were like family."

Chinook Centre provided an ideal atmosphere for growing a small business, say Jim and Keith Hannan of Keith's Deli.
Grant Black photo

year's worth of business in one month."

"It was an astronomical feeling," Forzani says, 30-plus years later. "As a retailer, when you have that first really big taste of success, you think maybe this is going to be something. Maybe this is going to be a real business."

Merchants throughout Chinook demonstrated that same spirit of entrepreneurship.

People were doing what they loved and "Chinook Centre was a very happy place," says Morley Sklar, the business ace behind British Boot Shops. "It was a place where people wanted to go to shop and where people wanted to go to work."

The British Boot Shop started at a downtown location, which Sklar bought and grew into a six-store family. Each store possessed a different atmosphere, decor and even different stock. Sklar opened his first British Boot Shop at Chinook in the 1970s, and soon afterwards unveiled a second store there for women. He would travel Europe, scouring the continent for the latest and greatest shoes and bags he could bring back.

"I loved it; I loved the business," Sklar says, still able to recall some of the specific merchandise he imported, including a $700 pair of Charles Jordan shoes

and the first offerings in Calgary of everything from Yves St. Laurent to Vans.

Local businesses were able to sell high-end merchandise largely due to the fact Calgary was home to so many oil companies, which generated wealth for many people, notes Sklar. "I had a woman come in; she'd been a customer for decades," he says. "There was a new shoe I had on display that had a beautiful ribbon around it. . . . She asked if it came in her size. . . . I said yes. It came in six different colours. She bought a pair in every colour."

Chinook Centre was indeed an ideal venue for independent businesses, says Keith Hannan, who opened Keith's Deli in the mall in 1972. "Chinook was a location where you could grow your business. . . . And, it was a place where friendships were formed," says Hannan, who was president of the Merchants' Association for one year and active on its board of directors for many more.

Keith's Deli became a popular spot for Calgarians, who savoured everything from Keith's corned beef and pastrami to homemade sausages. Years before shoppers could find roasted chickens for sale at their grocery stores, Keith was barbecuing chickens and roast beef for Calgarians, along with providing a menu of flavourful soups and sandwiches.

Reliable, good food was key. Customers

Community spirit ran high for merchants, especially during promotional events, such as Old Fashioned Days, celebrated here by Chinook Barber Shop staff, including (from left) Phil Streifel, Frank Patterson, Ken McEwen, Dennis Areschuck, Wally Senn, Maurice Noel, Stan Archambault and Pat Rica. Courtesy Phil Streifel

THE ABCs OF THE '70s

What trends and pop culture crazes impacted life in the 1970s? The Calgary Herald published this list:
- **A**didas, All in the Family, Alan Alda, Annie Hall, Afternoon Delight
- **B**ay City Rollers, beanbag chairs, the Bee Gees, the Blues Brothers, bell-bottoms, Barry Manilow
- **C**hokers, CB radios, convoys, caftans, The Carpenters, crockpots, Harry Chapin
- **D**isco Duck, disaster movies
- **E**ight-tracks, earth shoes, earthenware mugs, The Exorcist
- **F**arrah Fawcett, face lifts, Fame
- **G**et down, gold chains, Glen Campbell, garlic bread
- **H**all parties, Helen Reddy, house plants, The Hustle, herbal teas, Honda Civics
- **I**rish coffee, I Am Woman, I'm OK-You're OK, the Incredible Hulk
- **J**ack Nicholson, Jaws, jogging, Jonathan Livingston Seagull, John Travolta
- **K**ung fu
- **L**eisure suits, lava lamps, Looking for Mr. Goodbar, living together, love is never having to say you're sorry
- **M**artinis, Mary Tyler Moore, mood rings, macramé, Monty Python
- **N**uclear power, natural
- **O**livia Newton John
- **P**alazzo pants, pet rocks, place mats, Pearl Drops, ponchos, Pop Tarts, Pintos
- **Q**ueen
- **R**oller skating, roll-on lipgloss, Rocky
- **S**teak and lobster, ski sweaters, streaking, sheepskin seat covers, Sonny and Cher, Saturday Night Fever, Star Wars, shag haircuts and carpets, sideburns
- **T**owering Inferno
- **U**nited Nations
- **V**ans, vegetarians, Village People
- **W**ide ties, waterbeds, white suits
- **Y**oko Ono, yoga
- **X**erox colour copier
- **Z**its, Zowie Bowie

knew what to expect, even when it came to the featured soup. Wednesday was always a goulash, for example; Friday was seafood day, alternating between a red and white seafood soup each week.

Keith eventually moved his deli across the street from Chinook in 1998, as it became increasingly challenging for a small independent deli to operate in the growing mall. But the original spirit of Keith's Deli continues today in a location at 6100 Macleod Trail, run by Keith's son, Jim, and his wife, Wendy.

"Our food is something customers still want," says Jim. "As long as the quality is up, people will come."

"We have some customers who are 37-year customers," adds Keith. "Some have been here since day one in Chinook Centre."

Long-time customers were a source of pride for mall merchants, as was the fact that they worked together in Chinook to form a community. After their long days, many business owners and employees would gather to unwind, drink in hand.

"In that era, the bar was a big thing," says Karen Mottishaw, daughter of Roy Mottishaw, who owned some of the mall's first restaurants and lounges, including the Lamplighter Lounge.

"Dad had the most loyal bar following I ever saw," recalls Karen. "It was kind of like a Cheers atmosphere, where everybody knew everybody. . . . It was a comfortable place."

Roy, who also operated the well-known Tea Kettle Inn, had already made his mark as a restaurateur before Chinook. The Carolina restaurants he opened at the mall (there were three at one point) took his business to a new level. With his four daughters often working for him, Roy rose to the challenge of providing interesting dining experiences in the mall.

"He was aware of competition. . . . He always wanted to give customers something new or different," says Karen. "Renovating the restaurant was his passion," she adds, recalling his establishments took on several forms over the years, including The Copper Creperie and Casey's.

Peter and Rita de Graaf, owners of the Carolina Terrace restaurant, still possess and use some of the dishes from their restaurant 30-plus years later.   Grant Black photo

Roy passed away in 2008, but as Karen notes, "The whole Chinook Centre experience was very positive for him."

His expertise in the restaurant business was something he shared with many around him, including Peter de Graaf, who eventually bought the Carolina Terrace restaurant. De Graaf started at Chinook in the early '60s at the Alberta Piano Company, but eventually decided to give the restaurant business a try. He told Roy Mottishaw he would manage the Carolina for a month for free. After a month, if Mottishaw didn't like the job being done, de Graaf would leave. However, if he liked what he saw, de Graaf would get the job.

Mottishaw not only hired de Graaf; he ultimately encouraged his restaurant manager to buy the Carolina Terrace. Located beside the theatre, the Terrace grew in popularity, largely due to tasty specials such as chicken pot pie for $3.25 and apple strudel for 99 cents.

"Chinook Centre was always at the forefront of things, and thinking of the next great idea before it happened," says de Graaf's daughter, Patricia Stewart, who worked at the mall while attending school. "It was a great place for teenagers to find part-time work, and it was a great place for people to shop."

"Chinook became an entertainment centre, a gathering place where people could eat, go to movies or bowl," adds de Graaf, who also took a turn serving as president of the Chinook Merchants' Association.

Together, the merchants ran promotions and special events such as the aforementioned Old Fashioned Days, which are still talked about decades later. However, interest in the Merchants' Association faded as the decade drew to an end and the association eventually ceased operating years later. An increasing number of national and international chain stores were moving into the mall and the small-town feeling that once defined Chinook was beginning to morph into one of urban sophistication.

"Some things have changed at Chinook, while others stay the same," says de Graaf. "Years ago, Chinook was the place to go to, for shopping and dining, and I think it still is today."

"In the 55 years we've been here (in

Looking north towards downtown (seen in the distant background), construction of the Chinook-Ridge expansion was under way in April 1973. Calgary Herald Archive

Calgary and area), we've seen so much change," adds his wife, Rita de Graaf. "Calgary had a population of 170,000 when we arrived. . . . You can imagine what a difference Chinook Centre made in the city over the years."

During the 1970s, the mall itself underwent a major transition in operation. On Jan. 29, 1970, the owners of the Southridge Mall announced they'd purchased Chinook. Oxlea Investments, a real estate holding company for Edmonton's Oxford Leasehold group, now owned Calgary's largest mall.

Oxford's decision to acquire Chinook was an important step for the company, says Jon Love, whose father Don Love started Oxford in 1960. It was part of Oxford's early growth, which eventually included properties from coast to coast.

The deal was an amicable one. In Chinook's annual report, co-founder Reg Jennings said the sale was well received: "Your board welcomes the addition of Oxlea nominees to the Board of Directors of Chinook and anticipates the benefits from their advice and counsel."

Because an agreement was reached between Oxlea and the 16 Chinook shareholders who had controlling interest, changes would be minimal, the shopping centre said. Red Dutton would remain chairman of Chinook's board, Reg Jennings would continue on as president and Ken McGregor as mall manager.

Chinook's financial success was well documented in annual reports throughout the decade. The centre recorded increases in gross sales of up to 12 per cent in some years. As stores made more money, so too did Chinook. The centre's growing revenue came "directly from an increase in tenants' sales, thereby producing a greater percentage rental income," Jennings noted at the time.

In Chinook's first year of operation in 1960, it collected $800,000 in rental revenue. That figure had more than doubled to $1.69 million by 1970.

Once Chinook Centre and Southridge were both owned by the same company, speculation quickly grew about if, or when, the two malls would merge.

The two structures were separated by about 600 feet of parking space and one public street.

"The shopper flow between the two centres now, in all types of weather, warrants serious consideration of eventually linking the two malls," said Herald columnist Vern Simaluk in February 1970.

On May 10, 1971, Southridge and Chinook publicly announced they would indeed merge into one shopping centre to become Western Canada's largest mall. Its name would be Chinook-Ridge Centre, and it would feature the two malls' existing department stores, as well as 120 retail stores and professional services. The centre's site was now 52 acres in size, with free parking for 4,000 vehicles.

In an internal Oxford shifting of properties, Chinook-Ridge then acquired Southridge. It also bought smaller shopping centre properties, such as Northdale Shopping Centre in Manitoba and Waterloo Square Shopping Centre in Ontario.

Chinook-Ridge asked the city for permission to shut off 60th Avenue Southwest (the road running between the two malls.) If approved, Chinook-Ridge said it would expand and add new retail space and parking facilities. Both of the major department stores in the shopping centre, Woodward's and Simpsons-Sears, said they'd like to expand their stores if the malls were linked.

In June of 1972, debate continued at city hall about what to do with the area. Some council members, including Mayor Rod Sykes, were concerned about the mall's proposal to close the road that ran between the two structures. Overall mall expansion could be detrimental to the community and lead to decreased housing in the area, he feared.

However, council voted in favour of the mall's application to shut down the road. This also cleared the way for the city and Chinook to negotiate other land exchanges, road closures and realignments required for the Macleod/Glenmore interchange.

In spring 1973, Chinook-Ridge announced an expansion, also deciding it would keep a drive-through road open between the two malls on street level and build a bridge over the road.

"Customers will be able to walk and shop practically from 58th Avenue to 66th Avenue Southwest," manager Ken McGregor explained.

Changes at Chinook in the 1970s saw the mall's famous tower sign brought down, and its Chinook-Ridge moniker changed back to Chinook Centre.

The expansion project would not only consist of the bridge. It would also include 200,000 square feet of new space, 50 shops and a two-level parking structure with 720 more spaces.

At first, the marriage between Chinook Centre and Southridge wasn't easy for all merchants in the shopping centre. There was a bit of jealousy between retailers from the two previously independent centres. They'd been competi-

tors for five years and now they were expected to "play nice." It was a period of adjustment.

Mall owners also tried to convince Calgarians that the merged centre should be referred to as Chinook-Ridge, but the new name never stuck. On May 15, 1974, the name of the entire facility was changed back to Chinook Centre.

Chinook's expansion celebrated its grand opening the following day, May 16. The two mall structures, previously standing as separate buildings, were now connected by expanded wings leading

Artists' sketches show how the mall would be updated for the 1970s.   *Courtesy Chinook Centre*

to a second level bridge. The number of stores and services totalled 175.

The $5.5-million expansion gave Chinook room to welcome new shops, such as Tip Top, Fairweather, the Klothes Kloset and Shirt Shop, Toy House and Thrifty's. A number of stores achieving retail success elsewhere in Calgary also opened up shops in Chinook, including Riley & McCormick, Thom McAn Footwear, Classic Books, O.B. Allan Jewellers, Bowring gift shop, People's Jewellers, British Boot Shop and Dalmy's.

Popular merchandise on sale that day reflected trends of the times. Calculator World offered the numeric devices that everyone suddenly wanted and needed. A 12-feature calculator, selling for $100 to $200 elsewhere, was on

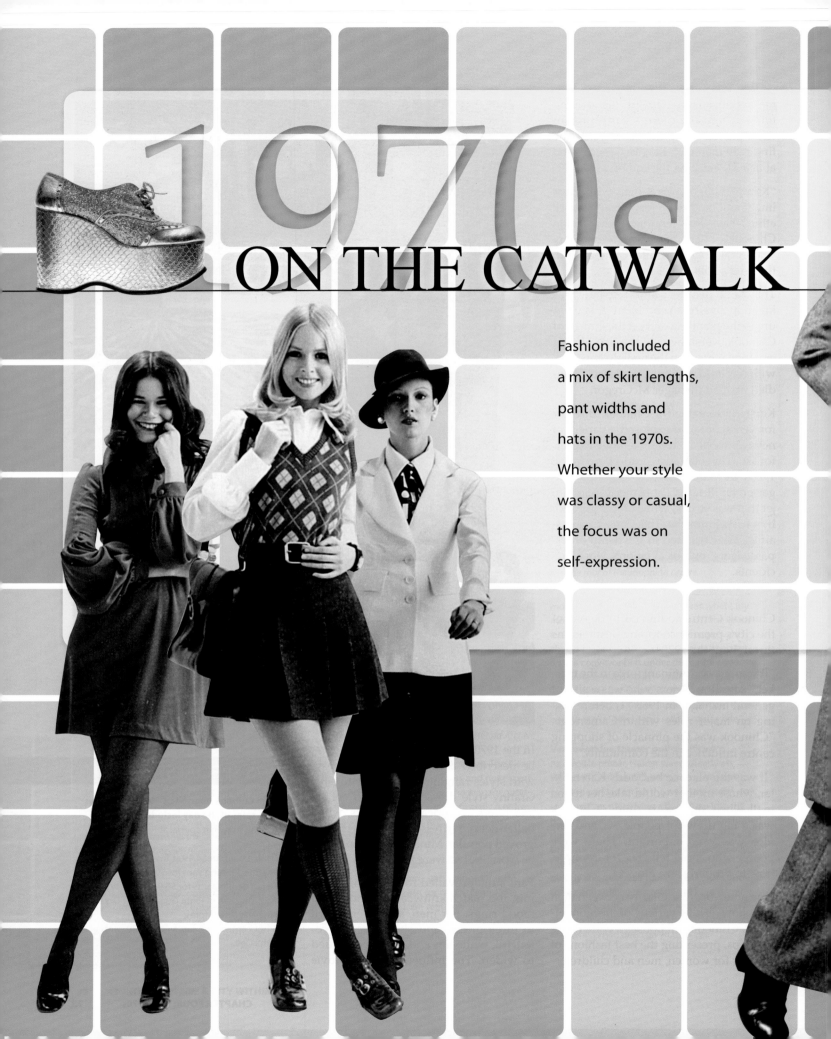

1970s
ON THE CATWALK

Fashion included a mix of skirt lengths, pant widths and hats in the 1970s. Whether your style was classy or casual, the focus was on self-expression.

Shoppers stroll in the newly expanded Chinook Centre in this May 1974 photo. The expansion linked the Chinook and Southridge shopping complexes with 30 new shops and stores, meaning it was now possible to reach all parts of the newly united malls without going outside.   Calgary Herald Archive

Saturday Night Fever grew and disco began impacting 1970s fashion, giving rise to gold fabrics, leopard prints, Lycra pants and increasingly high platform shoes.

Some of the "hippie" looks of the 1960s also carried into this decade, but by 1979, punk was king and leather jackets and straight-legged jeans were everywhere.

It wasn't just fashion that was changing in Calgary in the 1970s; the entire city was evolving. The decade proved to be a heady time, largely due to skyrocketing oil prices. The oil-rich area prospered as the world was rocked by energy crises, gas rationing and conflicts in the Middle East. Central Canadians began calling Albertans blue-eyed sheiks, in reference to the oil wealth generated here.

Battles began between Ottawa and the Alberta government, now led by Peter Lougheed. Ottawa wanted to control everything from oil exports to prices, which didn't sit well in Alberta. While Prime Minister Pierre Trudeau's popu-

larity grew in many parts of the country, Trudeaumania was a concept that never achieved liftoff in Alberta.

Tens of thousands of Canadians moved here, searching for work and riches. Between 1971 and 1981, Calgary's population alone grew by 50 per cent, to about 600,000. The city burst at the seams and development occurred everywhere, leading the construction crane to become known as Calgary's unofficial bird.

"The 1970s was the decade that brought big city status — and big city house prices — to Calgary," the Herald noted in 1979.

In 1971, 42 per cent of Calgary families could afford to purchase a new house. The city, with a population of 399,000, was one of Canada's most affordable. By 1979, however, the population leapt to 540,000 and house prices became the most expensive in the country. Only one-quarter of Calgary families could now afford a new home, with the average price jumping from $26,000 to $77,000 in those same years.

Despite housing concerns, there was

plenty to celebrate in the city. Calgary marked its 100th birthday in 1975 and also hosted the Grey Cup for the first time that same year. The world-class equestrian facility of Spruce Meadows opened its gates. The University of Calgary saw enrollment grow from 12,000 in 1971 to 20,000 in 1979. Local politician Joe Clark, of High River, became leader of the national Progressive Conservative Party in 1976, and in June 1979 began a nine-month stint as Prime Minister.

The decade ended on a high note, with optimism still being the order of the day. A group of local businessmen was getting closer and closer to the dream of bringing a National Hockey League team to Calgary. An impassioned bid committee was on the verge of convincing the International Olympic Committee that the city should host the 1988 Winter Games. Everywhere in Calgary jobs were plentiful, businesses were booming and retail spending intensified.

Few would have predicted that everything was about to come crashing down.

THEN . . .

Calgary Herald Archive

This view of Calgary's skyline, from the pedestrian bridge that leads to Prince's Island Park, shows the changes from 1972, above, to 2009.

. . . AND NOW

Grant Black photo

The 1988 Winter Olympics were a defining moment for Calgary, as the city welcomed the world and was thrust into the international spotlight. Here, the popular Olympic mascots Hidy and Howdy give a wave (left), while the opening ceremonies became a celebration to remember (above.)   *Calgary Herald Archive*

NHL President John Ziegler, left and Calgary Olympic boss Frank King drop the puck between Wayne Gretzky and Lanny McDonald on Oct. 15, 1983, the first game at the Saddledome.   *Calgary Herald Archive*

Life in Calgary, however, took a turn for the worse on Oct. 28, 1980. That's the day the federal government introduced the National Energy Program, designed to increase taxes on oil and control its price. While some parts of Canada would benefit from decreased oil prices, the energy-dependent economy of Alberta wilted. Thousands of Albertans lost their jobs, their homes and their savings, while businesses — small and large — were forced to close their doors.

"From 1979 to 1980, you couldn't do anything wrong," says Ken McCowan, owner of Thomas Jeffery menswear, which had a location in Chinook Centre from the mid-70s to 1990. Before the NEP, sales were healthy, customers were confident about the future and businesses thrived.

"When the NEP came down, it almost took us totally out of business. It was just like somebody shut off the spending valve," McCowan says.

Working in a province that experiences such economic extremes is memorable in both good times and bad, says Kip Woodward, who started work in the late 1970s at the family department store (Woodward's) in Chinook. "One thing I remember very clearly is the giddiness of the boom, and then the bust."

The 1980s quickly became a challenging economic period. The country sank into a recession, as did many other parts of the world. Interest rates, unemployment and inflation were all higher in Canada than in the U.S. Oil prices collapsed in 1986. Then, Black Monday hit on Oct. 19, 1987. Stock markets crashed around the globe, with American and Canadian markets taking dives of more than 22 per cent. At the time, it was the largest one-day percentage loss in history.

The economy wasn't the only factor leading to change at Chinook Centre;

THEN . . .

The Saddledome – the city's unique saddle-shaped arena – has become a defining architectural characteristic of Calgary. Above, construction of the 'Dome more than 25 years ago was necessary for Calgary to win the Olympic bid and to successfully bring an NHL team to town.   *Calgary Herald Archive*

. . . AND NOW

The food court (at top of photo) was considered a shopping centre innovation when first constructed in the early 1980s.

Photo courtesy Chinook Centre

mall ownership was about to transition, too. Chinook's owner, Oxford, included a division called Cambridge. Cambridge broke away from Oxford and became its own company under the leadership of J. Lorne Braithwaite. In 1981, Cambridge Shopping Centres bought Chinook Centre from Oxford.

"Cambridge was a small company at the time and Chinook was our largest property," recalls Braithwaite, then president and CEO of Cambridge. "Chinook was a great mall in a great location. It really helped us grow."

Throughout the 1980s, change remained a constant at Chinook Centre. New faces came on the scene and familiar friends passed. Chinook co-founder Reg Jennings died in 1982. His life-long business partner, Mervyn (Red) Dutton, passed away five years later. The two men had used foresight and business acumen to create and construct many of Calgary's landmarks, including Chinook Centre.

Meanwhile, the administration of Chinook Centre moved into the hands of a new mall manager, John Kennedy, who arrived at the start of 1982, just before the centre's new food court opened.

The concept of a food court was just be-ginning to become standard in malls, recalls Mike Mehak, who oversaw several changes to the centre, in roles with Oxford, Cambridge and then as a consultant. "There was very little new construction in Calgary due to the NEP, so the new food court was exciting," he says.

Despite the economic times, Chinook's owners wanted to ensure that the shopping centre didn't stand still and that it assertively grew its market share. Thus, Chinook continued to metamorphosize.

In October 1984, Chinook celebrated the fact that it finally closed the drive-through road that had divided the mall's main floor. "(Shoppers) had to go outside on the lower level and get through the traffic — you could say we used to be separated, somewhat," marketing director Ryck Bourgette said at the time. "But now, we are a city within a city."

The main level of the centre became completely enclosed, just like the second floor had been since the two former malls of Chinook and Southridge were joined in 1974. At the same time, the Safeway store that was located in the middle of the parking lot was moved inside.

Renovations in the 1980s included new entrances, glass installation, upgraded flooring, better lighting and a general sprucing up of the 25-year-old shopping centre.
Calgary Herald Archive

The renovations also resulted in additional space for new retailers and in upgrades, including new lighting, flooring and an all-glass entry for the addition on the west side. Bourgette noted that the mall now housed stores that carried fashion lines found on New York's Fifth Avenue, as well as shops that appealed to those on a modest budget. "We consider ourselves to be a family mall and cater to everyone's needs," he said. Stores now numbered 250 at Chinook, and with its 25th anniversary just one year away, the mall was making plans for upgrades to be complete as part of its celebrations.

At the same time, Chinook Centre went through the same growing pains every other shopping centre was experiencing over the issue of Sunday shopping. Chinook started a seven-day-a-week operation in October 1984 — a Canadian first.

Opening seven days a week was particularly challenging for independent retailers. Longer hours made it increas-

MEMORABLE MOMENTS

Barry Lammle, president and CEO of Lammle's Western Wear and Boutique of Leathers:
In the 1970s, Lammle — then the owner of two Boutique of Leathers stores — wanted to open a third location, this one in Chinook Centre. "There was always a waiting list of stores that wanted to open in Chinook," recalls Lammle, who was told a Chinook manager would check out his other stores before making a decision. The manager stopped by his downtown store one day while Lammle was out. However, Lammle's grey standard poodle was at the store that day, perched on a favourite spot on the store's staircase. When Lammle returned, he heard that the Chinook manager had been to the store and was less than impressed with the canine's presence. A short time later, the manager phoned him. "He said, 'I was in your store and I don't like dogs. And, I don't think dogs belong in a store. But, I do like your store and I want you in Chinook.'" Thus began Lammle's long-standing association with Chinook Centre.

Carmine D'Ambola, long-time barber and co-owner of Esquire Barber Shop:
"Over the years, the regular customers became more than customers. They became friends; they became good friends." Those friendships led D'Ambola to the bedside of first mall manager Ken McGregor, who wanted a hair cut while recuperating in hospital from a heart attack. He also gave trims to Chinook founder Red Dutton at the hospital and at home, after an accident left Dutton immobilized with a broken hip. "For those of us at Chinook, we were a community. You don't find that same kind of thing these days."

Karen Sklar, part of the family-run business British Boot Shop:
"On days like Boxing Day, it was like nothing you've ever seen. Back then, there weren't sales occurring all the time, like there are now. . . . So, when we had a sale at the shops, the crowds were unbelievable. We'd have to lock the doors and hire security guards. We couldn't let everybody in all at once."

Chinook Centre's marketing and promotional activities grew to include sponsorship of a chuckwagon at the Calgary Stampede. In 1989, chuckwagon driver Buddy Bensmiller (above) piloted the Chinook Centre rig to win the event and become champion on the Half Mile of Hell track.   Calgary Herald Archive

ingly difficult for small business owners to staff their shops and to find a work/home balance, says Ron Renaud, who managed the mall in the late '70s. It contributed to "the number of owner-operated stores decreasing. . . . There were fewer entrepreneurs."

As mall hours extended, it became harder to run a business, agrees Al Hardstaff, who operated Chinook Optical for 40-plus years. "It led to extra staff and extra costs. For many of the smaller guys, this meant when their leases came up, they left. I was one of the few who stayed."

After 14 months of opening on this extra day, however, Sunday became a strong performer, with a solid sales-per-hour figure. Those businesses that operated on Sundays outperformed those not open by as much as 30 per cent in overall sales for the entire week.

"It was very successful when we started in the fall of 1984 . . . (and) it got stronger and stronger as time went on," says John Kennedy. By 1986, "virtually the entire mall had subscribed to the seven-day advantage."

In 1985, as Chinook turned 25 years old, mall renovations continued with improvements made to lighting, floors and entrances. The shopping centre still had much of a $16-million to $22-million expansion remaining, which would be completed over the next two years.

The upgrading meant that by mid-1987, Chinook would be home to 42 new shops, 700 additional parking stalls and Brettons, a two-level department store, 45,000 square feet in size. Woodward's also spent about $2.5 million on its store, relocating almost every department.

On Aug. 26, 1987, Chinook opened this new expansion, totalling 70,000 square feet. New stores included Roots, Danier, Club Monaco, Benetton and Windriver Outfitting Company. The 700 new parking stalls brought the total number of spaces to 5,200. A parking structure with red iron spirals now sat at the front of Chinook Centre. At the back, a tunnel linked a parking area with Brettons, while a skywalk joined them on the second floor.

The focal point of the expansion, however, was on Brettons, a department store chain based out of Ontario. Smaller than traditional department stores, Brettons focused on high-quality, upscale merchandise. Labels found there on opening day included Hilary Radley, Simon Chang, Mexx and OshKosh B'Gosh.

"This was a major redevelopment," notes Kennedy. "It was an exciting new store for Calgary. The year 1987, however, wasn't a good time for retail. We had a successful opening . . . (but) the new stores didn't catch on."

With consumers hanging on to their money tighter than they did in the '70s, Chinook paid an increasing amount of attention to marketing events. These activities had already been important to the mall, but they became even higher profile throughout the decade.

Chinook sponsored, or became involved in, events ranging from the United Way bed races and clean river campaigns to downhill ski races and bridal shows. Special affairs at the mall included rose shows, African Violet displays, model searches, science fairs, self-defence demonstrations and concerts.

After a joint sponsorship with two other malls, Chinook began sponsoring its own chuckwagon at the Calgary Stampede each year, buying the tarp of Allan Bensmiller first, and then his son Buddy Bensmiller, who won the event in his Chinook Centre rig in 1989.

Chinook became very integrated within the city, says Ron Meiers, who was the assistant manager of the mall before eventually becoming chief operating officer of Cambridge. "It started way back with Chinook's early promotions. Those were ground-breaking things that no one else was doing. People really became connected to the shopping centre, which continues today. . . . Chinook is part of the fabric of the community."

All the special events at the shopping centre helped drive customers to the mall's stores, where fashion was chang-

The Chinook Centre Stampede Breakfast continued to prove popular, rain or shine. Calgary Herald Archive

Kids of all ages marvelled at Chinook's annual Christmas and Santa display. Calgary Herald Archive

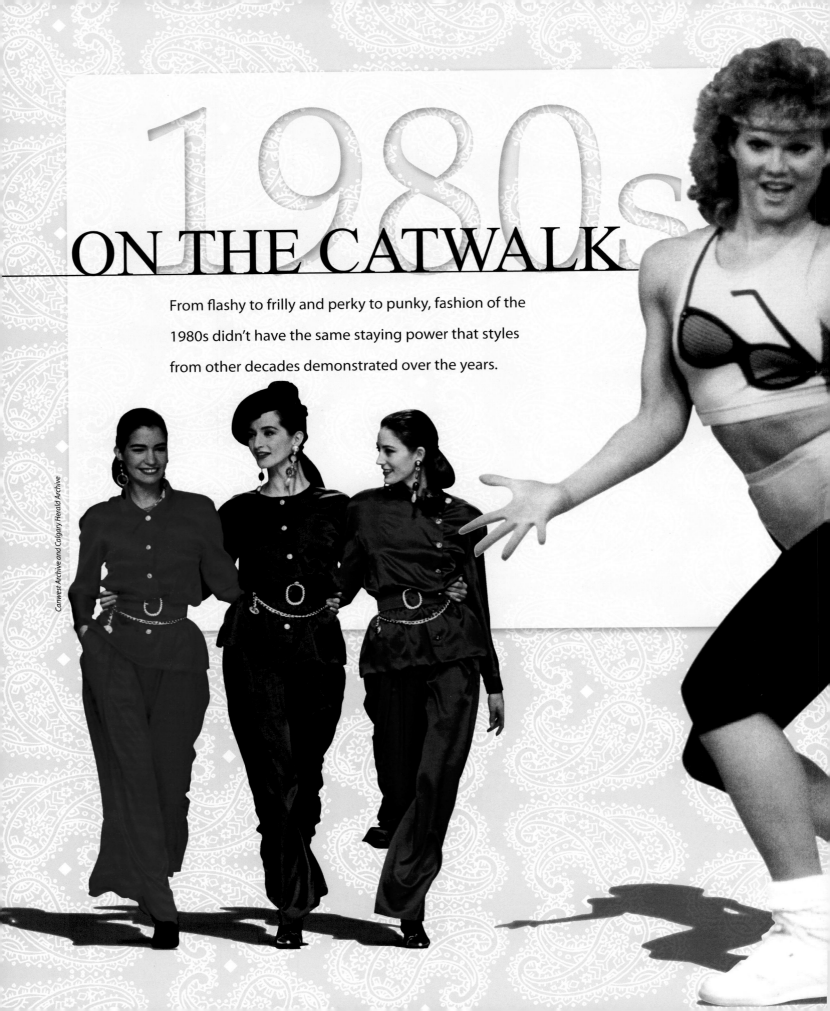

1980s
ON THE CATWALK

From flashy to frilly and perky to punky, fashion of the
1980s didn't have the same staying power that styles
from other decades demonstrated over the years.

J. Lorne Braithwaite, former president and CEO of Cambridge Shopping Centres:
"If you look at every major metropolitan area, there are two or three dominant malls that are centres of the community. . . . Chinook was one of those from the start."

Phil Streifel, long-time owner of Chinook Barber Shop:
"Some people have been coming to see us for haircuts for decades. We've given cuts to four generations of some families." Over the years, Streifel's routine has included picking up a couple of customers with disabilities or health problems and bringing them to the shop for haircuts. "You get to know these guys pretty well. They are indeed friends."

Maureen Karran, long-time Chinook Centre employee:
Taking care of financial and administrative duties in the days before computers was a challenge, Karran recalls. She'd sort boxes full of account payables, enter data in ledger books and manually balance sales reports from 200 stores. "I used to have dreams at night of numbers, numbers and more numbers," she laughs. Importantly, however, everyone who worked there was proud of Chinook." It was a real source of pride to say I worked at Chinook Centre. Still to this day, I feel privileged to say that I worked there. . . . Chinook was, and is, a part of the community."

Barb Sartison, Chinook Centre office administrator:
"The people who have managed the shopping centre, and the people who work there, are a big part of what makes the mall special. They care about Chinook Centre."

This 1987 photo shows the eye-catching red spirals of the vehicle ramp at Chinook Shopping Centre; the ramp was a visible sign of improved parking and traffic management. *Calgary Herald Archive*

ing faster than ever. Men were buying designer suits, with narrower lapels. For a more casual choice, the Miami Vice look ruled; guys started wearing jackets with T-shirts and pastel colours were plentiful.

For women, suits were the corporate choice of the decade and the bigger the shoulder pad, the more powerful the suit. The glitz seen in TV shows such as Dynasty and Dallas influenced evening apparel, while younger women's wear was impacted by the movie Flashdance and the Material Girl, Madonna. Ripped sweatshirts, leggings, loads of necklaces, headbands and lace gloves were big, as was the colour black.

The 1980s also saw the rise of acid wash jeans, denim jackets, digital watches, Ray-Ban sunglasses and the pastel polo shirts synonymous with the preppy look.

Merchandise in Calgary stores really began changing in the 1980s, says Din Peerani, owner of Formans Fashion Group. Peerani — who began working with Formans in 1977 before buying the menswear store in 1985 — noticed a pattern he wanted to change. "Customers would come in the store and the fathers would continue to buy clothing from us, but their sons didn't. . . . They wanted something different."

As a result, Peerani began importing menswear from Italy, Germany and France. "That's how we captured the next generation of the market," he says. "They didn't want the domestic fit that their fathers wore. They wanted European brands."

Formans eventually left the mall and with his son joining him in the business, Peerani relocated the store (now featuring both men's and women's fashion) to a heritage building in central Calgary.

"Chinook was a great mall," he says. "We enjoyed being there."

The retailers were vital to Chinook's prosperity, says Kennedy, recalling success stories of local businessmen such as Barry and Doug Lammle who opened the western wear store that bears their last name.

Barry owned a Boutique of Leathers store in Chinook before the brothers decided to open Lammle's Western Wear in the mall and at other locations in the city. Chinook provided a very positive atmosphere, with good traffic for retailers, says Barry. "It was definitely friendly. You knew half the people in the mall. You'd come to work half an hour early to have coffee with them. We'd do favours back and forth."

The centre evolved to become the ideal location for a flagship store, he notes. And, success at Chinook often became a harbinger of a chain's prosperity.

"It (the Chinook store) is one of our

Renovations including new trees, skylights and wood panelling led to a brighter and airier atmosphere at Chinook, as seen here in 1988.   Calgary Herald Archive

most important stores," he says of the Lammle's chain, which opened its 25th store in its 25th year of operations last year.

Warm sentiments about Chinook are shared by many who spent time there, says Maureen Karran, who was an employee from 1977 to 2004. The shopping centre was important to employees, retailers and many repeat clients.

"There were a number of regulars we'd see, such as the Breakfast Club (a group of morning regulars), the mall walkers . . . and the Hat Lady. She was an older lady, who dressed to the nines, and would go to the Terrace Restaurant," says Karran. "Everybody would come here, especially on a Saturday."

Chinook reaped the rewards of a 1988 influx of Olympic visitors, but storm clouds were forming on the horizon for the mall's longtime cornerstone — Woodward's. Loyal fans of the store had always enthused that the quality of Woodward's goods and its standard of service were unmatched. But in the 1980s, Woodward's began to stumble.

Once a department store darling, its stock prices had soared to $42 a share in 1972. Within two decades, that price plummeted to 11 cents.

Analysts said a number of factors hurt the chain, starting with the recession of the 1980s and rising interest rates. Labour problems in British Columbia also contributed, as did increased competition from specialty shops and the fact Woodward's never expanded to the extent other department stores did.

A dispute within the Woodward's family (between chairman Chunky Woodward and Woody MacLaren, a cousin who was company president) caused further problems and resulted in the store selling its real estate assets. Family fighting over stock and assets intensified. Cambridge eventually acquired Woodward's real estate holdings for $215 million in 1985, while Safeway bought Woodward's Food Floors in 1987.

In 1989, Chunky Woodward (grandson of the store founder) resigned from the Woodward's company, after being forced out by a financial alliance from Toronto. The store tried restructuring, but failure loomed in the next decade.

CHINOOK IN THE 1980s

SIGNS OF THE TIMES IN 1989

• Music World opens a location in Chinook (situated at the site of the former Safeway store, near Sears) in September 1989. The store announces it will not only sell records, cassettes and compact discs; it will also expand in a new direction – video sales.

• The Body Shop sells eco-friendly T-shirts for $9.95, with proceeds going to help save the rainforests.

• Flames fever sweeps the city as the hometown NHL team beats Montreal to win the Stanley Cup in 1989. At Chinook's Flames Sport Shop, every item emblazoned with a flaming C sells out within hours. A shipment of 300 caps is sold in 30 minutes.

• In April 1989, Chinook merchants and customers lament the announcement that a national goods and services tax (GST) will be implemented across the country, including Alberta, within two years.

• Sears Chinook Centre offers a Chinese food cooking class, focusing on preparing the dishes with a microwave oven.

• A walking club for men and women over 50 years of age starts at the mall.

CHINOOK CENTRE

JAN. 8, 1993
Woodward's lays off more than 1,100 employees in Alberta and B.C.

JULY 25, 1993
Woodward's at Chinook closes, following an earlier announcement that the Bay is taking over.

FALL 1993
Chinook's owner, Cambridge Shopping Centres, sells 50 per cent of the mall to the Ontario Teachers' Pension Plan.

MARCH 30, 1994
Brettons at Chinook is closed after its parent company is forced into receivership.

OCT. 27, 1994
Sears opens its renovated store; another reno follows fours years later.

1995
Speculation begins that Chinook Centre will undergo a massive renovation.

MARCH 26, 1997
Cambridge sells its remaining 50 per cent ownership of Chinook to the Ontario Teachers' Pension Plan.

MARCH 11, 1998
The Calgary Planning Commission approves a $150-million expansion and renovation of Chinook Centre.

CALGARY & AREA

FEB. 19, 1990
Alberta celebrates Family Day for the first time.

DEC. 17, 1990
The GST (Goods and Service Tax) becomes law, coming into effect Jan. 1.

JULY 7, 1991
A new provincial drinking law allows alcohol to be served on Sundays in bars and lounges where food is also available.

DEC. 14, 1992
Ralph Klein becomes Alberta's premier.

OCT. 10, 1995
Christine Silverberg becomes Calgary's police chief, making her the first female to hold the position in any major Canadian city.

JULY 2, 1996
Calgary's population hits 767,059.

OCT. 4, 1998
The Calgary General Hospital is imploded.

JULY 6, 1999
Crude oil prices recover after a soft first half of the year and flirt with $20 US a barrel.

1990s

Everyone loves a carousel. Attracting visitors both young and old, the carousel at Chinook Centre spins in its circular dance seven days a week. Spirited horses stand ready to gallop into kingdoms and adventures, limited only by the imagination. Hopping onto one of the brightly coloured saddles makes it easy to leave the worries of the world behind for a few minutes.

"The carousel is a traditional amusement park ride," says Jim Conklin, a guru in the business, who brought this merry-go-round to the mall. "It's something everybody loves, everybody can ride and everybody can enjoy."

Chinook's carousel has roots dating back to the 1930s; that's when the original machine powering this ride was built. Conklin Shows purchased it in the 1940s, using it in Quebec and Ontario before Chinook Centre became its home. Installing a carousel in the shopping centre gave a bit of a nod to Chinook's own history. A merry-go-round once sat on this site, as part of the family friendly entertainment at the Chinook Drive-In.

More significantly, perhaps, the carousel reflects the change Chinook has experienced over the years. As almost every store and feature in Chinook has moved and/ or been renovated, so, too, has the carousel. It initially was installed outside the Bay, but was relocated, at the end of the 1990s, to its current location in the Food Court. This merry-go-round has undergone other changes, as well.

When it arrived, the ride's motif boasted wagon wheels and fence posts, reminiscent of a Wild West theme. These days, however, the carousel has matured and its outer ring of horses celebrates the provinces of Canada. Symbols of each province are lovingly hand painted on each horse's saddle.

PENNY WISE

The recently implemented GST meant that in January 1991, pennies were once again in demand. While most prices over the years had been rounded off to nickels and dimes, the new seven-percent tax had most items ringing up at odd-numbered prices. The result? Many stores were running out of pennies each day because they needed so many more when making change.

Some stores, however, dropped their prices to cut down on the need for pennies. The Second Cup coffee shop, for example, dropped the price of a medium coffee from 80 cents to 79 cents, so that when the GST was added, the price was 85 cents instead of 86.

Grant Black photos

The carousel is now a bit more grown up and a bit more sophisticated — much like Chinook itself.

While growing up, however, there are always bound to be some challenges. In 1990, as Canada went into another recession, those growing pains were felt by businesses across the country, especially by the once mightiest-of-the-west department store chain, Woodward's. Founded between 1891 and 1892, the company's 100th anniversary was marred by the fact it was forced to seek credit protection in 1992. Accumulated debt had skyrocketed to $65 million. Its share price had plummeted to 11 cents.

The store tried to salvage itself. In January 1993, Woodward's laid off 82 people at its three Calgary locations, including Chinook. At the same time, the store closed many of its favourite departments including furniture, appliances, electronics, fabrics, carpets, hardware, stationery, sporting goods, toys and restaurant operations.

The restructuring, however, didn't work and the Bay took over the chain in April 1993. Woodward's called it a "merger plan," that would see 21 of 25 Woodward's stores in Alberta and B.C. become a Bay or Zellers store. The Chinook location would be split into two separate stores – one Bay and one Zellers.

Increased competition from smaller stores and changing shopping habits – which saw people spend less in department stores – really hurt Woodward's, says Kip Woodward, great grandson of the store's founder.

"Department stores had really created the shopping centre. . . . Every centre had at least one department store anchoring one end of the mall, and probably a grocery store anchoring another end," says Woodward. "Their popularity, however, declined."

On July 25, 1993, Woodward's closed its doors at Chinook and long-time customers and employees mourned the loss.

"People were very loyal to Woodward's," says long-time Chinook employee Maureen Karran. "It was a big adjustment for many people to realize Woodward's wasn't going to be there anymore."

MEMORABLE MOMENTS

Al Pettigrew, carousel operator (at right):
"It's the kids that make this job. It's wonderful to see the looks on their faces, especially when you see them daydreaming. . . . When they look at you after they've had a ride and they say thank you, it's just heart-warming," says Pettigrew, a part-time operator at Chinook Centre's carousel. Pettigrew's also seen his share of older folks enjoy the carousel.
"We had one woman who was 82 years old. I got a chair to help her get on a horse. It was the first time she'd been on a merry-go-round."

Business

Editor: Ronald Nowell 235-7485

Saturday
July 24, 1993

The '70s were golden years for Woodward's. The chain was riding high in the marketplace — and profitable.

But customer loyalty failed to sustain the regional chain when markets changed and profits vanished

By Anne Crawford
Calgary Herald

END OF AN ERA: The Woodward's at Chinook Centre closes its doors for the last time on Sunday evening

Mike Sturk, Calgary Herald

THE DECLINE & DEATH OF A DEPARTMENT STORE

n the end, Woodward's didn't stand a chance.

It was beaten in a cutthroat industry by its small size, geographical location in boom-or-bust Western Canada, and its own mistakes and mismanagement.

Once the dazzling darling of investors and consumers — its share price in 1972 was $42 while sales shot exponentially off the page — the department store chain hit the '80s and started to stumble.

It was slammed by the recession and failed to respond to changes in the retail market. A Woodward family feud in the mid-'80s resulted in the sale of its real estate assets.

Later it sold its Food Floors.

Meanwhile, the family influence declined. In 1989 Chunky Woodward, grandson of the founder and chairman, was forced out and resigned.

Under new management, Woodward's made bright and brash promises. But, inevitably, the prolonged recession took its toll.

The company asked for court protection last December, weighed down by an accumulated debt of $60 million. Its share price was 11 cents when its trading on the Toronto Stock Exchange was halted.

Attempts to find a way to survive on its own proved futile and in April of this year it announced a "merger plan" with The Bay. The deal was approved in May and calls for the conversion of 21 of 25 Woodward's stores throughout Alberta and British Columbia to The Bay or Zellers.

Founded in 1892 in Vancouver, Woodward's celebrated its 100th birthday last year.

The department store chain first came to Calgary in 1960, as the anchor in the new Chinook Centre in the southwest. It was an immediate success in a growing suburban market.

In 1971 Woodward's opened a second store at Market Mall in northwest Calgary and its third store, at Sunridge Mall, opened in 1981.

During the '70s Woodward's was considered one of the most profitable department stores in Canada, outstanding for its strong customer loyalty. Not only that, but revenues soared.

At that time they were talking about buying Simpson's, recalls retail analyst John Winter of Toronto.

"An expansion East would have balanced the books," he says. "But it was a cash cow and they milked it. They took the profits and didn't invest to guarantee their future."

In the early '80s, Woodward's fell behind, Winter says. He recalls visiting a Woodward's store and seeing merchandise piled on trestle tables.

"I questioned their merchandising acumen, or lack of it."

Woody MacLaren, president of the company and a cousin of Chunky's, blamed the recession, labor unrest in B.C. and rising interest rates for Woodward's struggle during this period.

Then in 1985, he announced a deal to sell Woodward's real estate to Cadillac Fairview Corp. of Toronto.

In the midst of it, MacLaren launched a suit against Chunky, claiming he had an option to buy Chunky's family block of shares — 25 per cent of the company.

Chunky denied existence of the option and, while legal proceedings churned on, the two cousins faced off in a bidding war for Woodward's

real estate, with MacLaren on Cadillac Fairview's side, and Chunky backing Cambridge Shopping Centres Ltd.

Finally, the cousins settled out of court, while Cambridge won the bidding war, paying $215 million for the real estate, and Woodward's became a tenant rather than a landlord.

Many analysts point to the real estate sale as the beginning of the end.

"It's very difficult to run a retail chain without assets," Winter says. "When you have no assets, you have no equity."

The sale of the Food Floors to Safeway in 1987 spelled the "writing on the wall," he adds.

Stripped of its assets, Woodward's had no safety net. And times weren't getting better.

Its revenues, which peaked at $1.1 million in 1986, were plunging downward. In 1987, revenues were $815 million, including $127 million from the Safeway sale.

Both years it recorded net losses — $7.7 million or 45 cents a share in 1986 and $1.8 million or 10 cents a share in 1987, the latter bolstered by the $127-million infusion.

In 1989 it lost $59 million or $3.10 a share on revenues of $797 million.

That was the year Chunky was forced to give up control of the chain to a financial alliance from Toronto. Cambridge president Lorne Braithwaite took over as chairman and Hani Zayadi, formerly of Zellers, became president and chief executive officer.

The new broom tried to sweep clean.

There were layoffs and a repositioning back to the "old" Woodward's. The company reported good news — a three cents a share profit — for 1990.

But it was a blip. And it was all downhill from there.

In modern retail terms, Woodward's was just too small and too concentrated to survive, says Winter.

George Hartman of BBN James Capel in Toronto points out Woodward's annual revenues were down to roughly $600 [...] plus for Eaton's [...] failure to ex[...] substance to c[...]

"If it had b[...] ter and transf[...] said.

Woodward's [...] changes.

As the trend[...] at one end of the [...] at the other, Wo[...] trying to be all th[...] analyst Carl Hoyt [...]

In 1986, after fil[...] ing costs, the comp[...] sion-proof shopper [...]

It would put em[...] fashion, and reduce [...] and home furnishing[...]

By 1988, they we[...] around, which didn't [...] um market and stron[...] shops.

"Their attempts to r[...] late," Winter says.

Hoyt says that in[...] market, Woodward's e[...] with Eaton's and The Ba[...]

"They had no chance.[...]

Salespeople, shoppers lament loss of familiar atmos

he cool chrome, glass and marble of Woodward's cosmetic department is an oasis in the midst of dishevelment and desolation.

All around it, on what is left of Woodward's first floor at Chinook Centre, stand clothes racks, surrounded by hordes of deal-seeking consumers.

Cosmetics, with its exotic and expensive products and elegant look, is the only department left untouched by Woodward's final liquidation sale.

There are no 80-per-cent-off signs here.

Just a polished staff, embarrassed by the junk-store atmosphere, taking orders by phone because their regular customers won't come near the place.

"It's sad," they say, looking with relief to Sunday at 5 p.m., when the store closes its doors for good and the Woodward's story in Calgary comes to an end.

Loyal Woodward's shoppers, spotted among the bargain hunters, share the sadness.

Kathy Schiffner from Strathmore, combing racks of women's wear, said her mother had been a regular shopper in the store but "won't come in to see it looking this way."

"I'm sad to see it go," said Lyla Burns, who moved here from Ontario many years ago. She's furnished five houses in Calgary, using Woodward's as one of her favorite sources.

"It always had quality in things the other stores don't have."

Quality and service built the renowned Woodward's customer loyalty, according to dismayed last-minute shoppers.

"Everybody's upset," said one couple. "We've shopped here for years, since our kids were small. The quality was good and the price was good."

Irene Kohuch, a seven-year employee, said Woodward's has been a great company to work for. "It has a lot of loyal, dedicated employees and a lot of old customers who are devastated."

But morale has been bad over the last six months, as friends were let go and rumors ran rampant, said one cosmetics saleswoman, asking not to be named.

"It can only go up from here," she said. "People were rude to us. It almost felt like it was our fault."

The once-prestigious Chinook store is the last Woodward's outlet in the city to close.

It had already shrunk to little more than half its original size, with 100,000 square feet — two levels at the south end

— boarded up for [...]

The same conv[...] is happening at[...] Sunridge Mall.

At Market Mall, [...] on two levels, of [...] 200,000 square feet [...] to Zellers. The remai[...] devoted to new retail [...]

Two levels at [...] Woodward's at Sun[...] total of 114,000 square[...] Zellers. The leftover s[...] to extend the mall into [...] ment-by-department [...]

All three Zellers stor[...] to open Sept. 20.

The one new Bay st[...] will close for just [...] Renovations will contin[...] ment-by-department [...] reopening.

The cosmetic saleswom[...] of her colleagues in the [...] have new jobs with The Ba[...]

And while they're pleas[...] and the fact the compan[...] Canadian hands, they wish [...] could have stayed in its ol[...] stressing quality, service [...] loyalty.

"Cutting staff was disas[...] one.

"Customers like famili[...]

Herald Graphic

WHAT WILL BE BUILT WHERE WOODWARD'S WAS?

At Chinook Centre:

Zellers on upper level	The Bay on upper level
Zellers on lower level	The Bay on lower level

North

Woodward's has occupied space in Chinook Centre since 1960. Splits into Zellers on the south end and The Bay on the north end, both on two levels.

At Market Mall:

Zellers on upper level	Offices on upper level
Zellers on lower level	Retail on lower level

Southwest — Northeast

Woodward's has occupied space in Market Mall since 1971. Little more than half on the southwest end becomes Zellers, on two levels, while remaining space is devoted to retail downstairs and office space upstairs.

At Sunridge Mall:

Zellers on upper level	Mall expansion
Zellers on lower level	Mall expansion

South — North

Woodward's has occupied space in Sunridge Mall since 1981. Two levels at the south and become Zellers, while north end will be used to expand the mall entrance.

Opening Dates: The Bay opens August 9, under ongoing renovations. All three Zellers stores open September 20.

Source: The Bay and mall developers

The closure of Woodward's in 1993 was a major change for Chinook Centre, which had been anchored by the department store since the shopping centre's opening in 1960.

BOWLADROME LEVEL

Chinook Bowladrome 14

TO LOWER LEVEL

58 AVENUE S.W.

Woodwyn 169

Consumer Distributing 178A

Flinders Drugs 178

Metropolitan 172

Sears 187

Bretton's 199

Woodward's 132

Canada Safeway 133

GLENMORE TRAIL

LOWER LEVEL

5 STREET S.W.

Paul Squires, a former Woodward's manager, displays an archived proof of a $1.49 day ad that is a quarter of a century old. Specials of the day included 15 Valencia oranges, a package of 18 donuts and a slice of butter pecan pie garnished with fresh whipped cream , each for $1.49.

Grant Black photo

MEMORABLE MOMENTS

Paul Squires, a manager at Woodward's in Chinook:
The Breakfast with Santa was a notable part of the holiday season. Children would be treated to cartoons in the Chinook Theatre, be entertained by Buckshot, have breakfast in the Macleod Room at Woodward's and, finally, get a visit from Santa. "Woodward's was connecting to kids in the community," says Squires. That connection was further nurtured during the Cub Car Rally that the store hosted for years. Cubs and Scouts would carve toy cars out of a set provided by Woodward's and then race the cars on a track set up by the store. "Hundreds would come out for this," Squires recalls. "It was quite a bit of fun."

Hart Abercrombie, one of the original owners of Stephen Avenue Soup Co.:
"I think Stephen Avenue Soup Co. became a meeting point for people in the mall. We had a regular group of seniors who would meet there five or six days a week. We had Chinook employees who would stop in regularly for coffee — we all were close. It was an easy place to sit and have a meeting."

Barry Styles, former CEO of Highwood Communications:
"I remember when I was a customer of Chinook's, long before I worked on their advertising and marketing. I can remember when Woodward's was *the* gourmet store. One of the things that

was unique was they had a gourmet spice section. I didn't know what most of the spices were until I browsed through that section. . . . The main dining room that overlooked the mall was also a big attraction. . . .They had a twist on a steak sandwich; they served it on cheese bread, and the steak was shaved. It was fantastic."

Paul Brandt, country music star:
"Chinook Centre has been an icon of Stampede breakfasts over the years. I remember performing in that parking lot to syrupy-faced kids and their orange-juice toting parents when my career was first taking off. I ate my share of pancakes there, too. . . . A tip of the hat to Chinook Centre for 50 great years in the community."

Shopping at Woodward's had become a regular part of many Calgarians' lives, says Paul Squires, who was the manager in charge of advertising and displays at the Chinook store. "We would see the same families each week or month, and after a number of years we would see children from those families, who were now grown, coming to the store with their own families."

Because Squires spent a significant amount of time on the floor of Woodward's, he remained very recognizable to customers, even after the store closed. "People still want to talk to me about Woodward's and tell me they miss it. . . . One thing people really remember is $1.49 day. The sales were great. . . . People would line up outside the door. There'd be a mad dash to run to the various departments. . . . People loved it."

Adds long-time Chinook merchant Al Hardstaff, "Woodward's was a unique department store in Calgary and Chinook Centre. When it closed, it was like losing a limb. It was the biggest change the mall could have experienced."

The new anchor stores replacing Woodward's, however, said they were excited by the opportunity to better serve Calgarians.

"The Bay has been a major player in Calgary long before Woodward's ever was in the marketplace," said Bob Peter, the president of the Bay at the time, while visiting the new Bay and Zellers stores in Chinook Centre.

The '90s were an interesting time for Calgarians. A recession led people to watch their spending, while the city and province sought to diversify the economy.

The Conservatives continued to govern Alberta, but a new leader was at the helm – Ralph Klein. He worked to bring the province's financial house into better order and that meant spending cuts, much to the dismay of some people. His inimitable style, however, won him fans, leading him to become a dominant figure in politics throughout the decade.

In the 1990s, Calgarians were abuzz over several issues including fluoridation of

The 1990s saw Ralph Klein elected as premier, shown at top in his campaign office at Chinook Centre. The decade was also marked by two Grey Cup victories for the Calgary Stampeders (here, quarterback Doug Flutie holds the cup); the creation of the Calgary-based WestJet airlines; and, the opening of the Chinese Cultural Centre.   Calgary Herald Archive

Chinook's community outreach continued with events that included the well-known Benny the Bookworm sale, held to benefit the Calgary Philharmonic Orchestra, and an annual back-to-school event that resulted in supplies being collected for needy students.

Calgary Herald Archive

CLOSING TIME

Farewell, Library

When Chinook Centre opened in 1960, it was the place to be for any and all types of businesses and service providers, including the Calgary Public Library. However, use of the Chinook library branch decreased over the years. Some believed its low-profile presence in the lower part of the mall was a problem and the library decided to close its doors. Chinook Centre tried to keep the branch in the mall by offering the library alternate locations.

The shopping centre also said it would create a $2.7-million, 15,000-square-foot facility and rent it back to the library for $11 per square foot annually.

The library board responded this wouldn't be the best use of its limited resources and closed the branch in 1998.

Curtains for the Chinook Theatre

The 718-seat Chinook Theatre closed on Sept. 16, 1990, after a screening of Taking Care of Business. The theatre's lease had expired and the property was slated for redevelopment. Famous Players Ltd. had operated the theatre since its opening in May 1965. The closure left only one other single-auditorium first-run movie theatre in Calgary, at North Hill.

the drinking water; an LRT extension northwest to Brentwood Station; and, new smoking rules for the workplace.

The city saw Air Canada take over the Calgary-based Canadian Airline and witnessed WestJet fly into town; the Chinese Cultural Centre opened; and the Stampeders won the Grey Cup in 1992 and 1998. People also marvelled at Canadian girl power, with Celine Dion, Alanis Morissette and Shania Twain winning Grammy Awards within a year.

The decade was also a time of continuing layoffs in the oilpatch, with 700 people losing their jobs at Petro-Canada in the mid-'90s, along with 500 at Gulf and 400 at Nova, just to name a few of the larger downsizing moves.

Economic challenges led to a number of businesses closing at Chinook and other malls. Gone from the mall were Kresge's, Grafton & Co., Toys and Wheels, Big Steel, Dalmys, Antels, Cactus, Kinney, Marks & Spencer Canada Inc. and Easy Street. Also leaving was Brettons. The junior department store had worked hard to become an integral part of Calgarians' lives, doing everything from running regular skin care and make-up seminars to hosting a variety of talks on topics ranging from bonsai plants to handbags. However, its parent company Etac was forced into receivership and Brettons closed its doors in 1994.

Another significant change at Chinook in 1994, however, was the arrival of a new manager — the straight-shooting Terry Napper. Calm, composed and community-focused, Napper quickly became known for his unflappable and level-headed style of management.

"Terry tells it as it is, whether it is good news or bad news. Everyone appreciates that and respects that," says Barb Sartison, Chinook's office administrator, adding Napper's accessibility to retailers is also noteworthy. "If they have a question or a problem, Terry is there. He makes his own appointments. He sees everyone who wants to see him."

Napper quickly gained the respect of merchants and neighbours, says Al Hardstaff, who in addition to being the former owner of Chinook Optical, also lives in the adjacent Meadowlark Park. "Terry reached out to the community and built stronger ties between Meadowlark Park and Chinook Centre."

Throughout the 1990s, Chinook continued to grow its ties in the community. It started an annual Back to School Supply Drive that saw customers and merchants fill a school bus with thousands of dollars in supplies for needy students.

For many years, the shopping centre was home to the Benny the Bookworm event, a large second-hand book sale that raised funds for the Calgary Philharmonic Orchestra. And, Chinook's Charity Bazaar, benefiting dozens of local religious and community groups, continued until the late '90s.

The shopping centre continued on its path of being a gathering place for community members making a difference. Here, country musician George Fox gives autographs to fans, after performing songs from a CD that saw proceeds donated to Calgary Urban Projects Society.

Calgary Herald Archive

Chinook's popularity with shoppers continued to grow over the decades, says Hart Abercrombie, who — with partner Nick deHaam — opened his first business in the mall with a malt shop outside Woodward's in 1972. From there, the two men brought an outlet of their Stephen Avenue Soup Co. to the mall, followed by New York Fries.

"A lot of the mall's growth had to do with location," says Abercrombie. "But Chinook also grew its popularity with all its special events and promotions over the years. . . . Other malls eventually began to do the same kind of thing, but Chinook really did a good job of it."

The 1990s also saw ownership changes at Chinook Centre. By July 14, 1992, Chinook's owner, Cambridge, was controlling properties across the country including 30 regional shopping centres.

"The best way to describe Cambridge is (it is) the best horse in a very muddy race," president Lorne Braithwaite said at an annual meeting that year, in answer to a question about how Cambridge was faring in challenging economic times.

Cambridge looked for new ways to grow and prosper, which led to a relationship with the Ontario Teachers' Pension Plan. In fall 1993, Cambridge sold 50 per cent of Chinook Centre to the pension plan.

However, the two companies couldn't quite agree on what to do with Chinook Centre. The shopping centre was now more than 30 years old and various expansions over the years left the mall needing a renovation to make it more cohesive.

The Ontario Teachers group wanted a full-scale renovation, while Cambridge was interested in a moderate approach. Cambridge also wanted to move forward with a major reno at another mall it owned, Southcentre, which is located a few kilometres down Macleod Trail from Chinook.

BORN IN THE 1990s

A large number of inventions burst onto the scene in the '90s, changing the way we lived, shopped, played and worked.

• **1990:** World Wide Web invented by Tim Berners-Lee.

• **1990:** Rollerblades created.

• **1993:** Beanie Babies are born.

• **1995:** The $2 coin, the toonie, introduced in Canada.

• **1995:** Amazon.com and eBay come on the scene; the Sony PlayStation is also introduced.

• **1996:** Palm Pilot and DVDs go on sale.

• **1996:** Calgary-based WestJet is born.

• **1996:** Tickle Me Elmo is the new "it" toy.

• **1997:** First successful MP3 player invented.

• **1997:** J.K. Rowling's Harry Potter and the Philosopher's Stone is published in the U.K.

• **1997:** Google is invented, as is wi-fi wireless networking.

This artist's conception of Chinook Centre in the 1990s demonstrated how the redevelopment would impact the exterior of the mall.   *Calgary Herald Archive*

The result was that in February 1997, Ontrea (a real estate arm of the pension plan) gave notice that Cambridge needed to either buy the mall back, or sell its 50 per cent interest to Ontrea. Cambridge sold its share in Chinook and four other Canadian shopping centres to Ontrea for $315 million.

"When Teachers first bought into Chinook, we bought a package of malls from Cambridge — we had 50 per cent ownership," explains Bob Bertram, executive vice-president, investments, for the Ontario Teachers' Pension Plan.

The plan's executive, however, became concerned when Cambridge wanted to develop a competing mall on Macleod Trail, possibly to Chinook's detriment.

"It wasn't that Cambridge had written off Chinook; they just saw more redevelopment potential and had more land for redevelopment at Southcentre," says Bertram. "We saw the potential of Chinook, so we made them an offer. We bought all of Chinook.

"Chinook is located at the intersection of major arteries," he notes. "It's close enough to downtown to attract people from there. It has a big catchment area.

We felt it deserved to be redeveloped."

The Ontario Teachers' Pension Plan "definitely wanted to own that asset," adds Andrea Stephen, a former real estate director of the plan and now executive vice-president of investments for Cadillac Fairview.

"Calgary is such a great market," Stephen says, noting the city's growth has been remarkable.

"The potential for Chinook, at the time, was significant . . . but the mall was quite disjointed. We wanted to own the whole thing so we could embark on a unified renovation," she recalls.

Ontario Teachers initially hired 20 Vic Management Inc. to oversee the redevelopment and leasing of Chinook, but shortly after completion bought Cadillac Fairview. That company, a wholly owned subsidiary of Ontario Teachers, eventually came to own and manage about 80 commercial properties — including Chinook — for the pension plan.

Chinook presented an opportunity to transform into a best-in-class retail destination, says Peter Sharpe, president and CEO of Cadillac Fairview.

"While it enjoyed a prime location in Calgary, it needed a significant investment to broaden the retail offering and inject new life and energy," he says.

"This investment began in 1998 with a $200 million redevelopment that was completed in 2001. This commitment to quality and innovation at Chinook continues to attract unique, first-to-market retailers from across North America and Europe to the city," says Sharpe. "Chinook Centre is one of Cadillac Fairview's crown jewels and Calgary's premier shopping centre. The property has evolved significantly since it was first built in 1960 and continues to grow."

The late 1990s redevelopment was needed to improve the layout of the mall, but there were some concerns from the neighbouring community of Meadowlark Park about the expansion, recalls former alderman Barry Erskine.

Neighbours didn't want to look at a bunch of blank walls at the back of a building, he said. It was a sentiment that led Erskine to help facilitate meetings between the mall and the community. Design plans were discussed and eventual consensus was reached to ensure there were buffer zones and that the mall's exterior included interesting storefronts.

"(Manager) Terry Napper was able to explain what Chinook needed to do and why," recalls Erskine. "And if he couldn't meet some of the demands of the community, he explained why. He was honest and straightforward and the community appreciated it. . . . What they did at the end of the day was they built a community."

During redevelopment, 120 stores were open, offering up fashions of the decade. There was the grunge look, featuring loads of flannel shirts. The Goth look became hot for both genders, with punk trends also continuing to reign for men.

Women took to piercing their belly buttons, wearing matte lipstick and using scrunchies in their hair. Classic blazers, long and straight, were the No. 1 choice for work, while pink emerged as an "it" colour for females.

DISCOVER Chinook

Winter 1998

CHINOOK CENTRE

Sign *of the* Times

Chinook Centre stands tall and proud in the heart of Calgary

When Calgarians look back on their history 50 years from now, the economic excitement of the 1990s could be the conversation spur.

This decade has seen immense growth, with numerous major corporations across North America relocating their head offices or creating a presence in Calgary. No longer is this city referred to as the "best-kept secret" in the country.

Calgary, by virtue of its highly talented and educated workforce, is on the leading edge of research and development with local scientists receiving international recognition.

As we approach the new millennium, Calgary has one of the most dynamic economies in the country.

And as the city grows, so grows the vitality of its retail community. When it comes to expansion, this city has never been shy to jump at opportunities.

In 1960, a group of prominent Calgary businessmen joined to develop Chinook Centre—a bold venture that created more than 1,000 jobs and placed this city in the shopping forefront of Western Canada.

Today, 38 years later, Chinook Centre stands tall and proud in the heart of this city and in a prime location at the intersection of Macleod and Glenmore Trails.

More than 174,000 cars pass by Chinook each day and, last year, more than 13 million people visited the Centre, spending in excess of $250 million.

Calgary's success, along with Chinook's incredible track record, provides solid reasons for the centre's current $150 million redevelopment program.

With the additional retail stores, larger food court, increased parking and the streetscape effect, it's not hard to understand Chinook General Manager Terry Napper's reference to the centre as "Calgary's mall."

Two of the Centre's anchor stores—Sears and Zellers—have already undergone major renovations while, next year, Chinook will introduce several new retailers including Calgary's largest Banana Republic store, which will occupy some 7,000 sq.ft.

The full renovations are expected to be completed in November, 1999.

In true Chinook Centre style, it's business as usual and more than 120 stores have been operative through the current renovation period.

Like the bold thinking that launched Chinook 38 years ago, the Chinook redevelopment is part of the Calgary way—Calgarians see a need and implement a solution.

And when that discussion on Calgary's history is held 50 years from now, Chinook Centre will, without question, be featured.

Meanwhile, "Calgary's mall" will be preparing for the next Millenium.

Inside

Fashion 3
Charity 4
New Look 5
History 6-7

Big Sky Big Country Big City Big Change
CHINOOK

OFFICE

ROTUNDA

WEST ENTRY

WILSONS

NOVA

CAFE

EXPRESS

KIDS

BEAUTY

CALGARY HERALD
A Calgary Herald special advertising feature

The redevelopment of Chinook Centre would provide the shopping centre with a new sophistication and easy-to-navigate floor plan.   *Calgary Herald Archive*

1990s
ON THE CATWALK

When it came to fashions of the decade, khaki rocked, grunge was cool, casual Fridays ruled and suits were sophisticated or sassy.

CHINOOK CENTRE

CALGARY & AREA

Canwest Archive, Calgary Herald Archive, and stock.xchng

JAN.13, 2000
City planning commission gives approval for a 4,000-seat multiplex theatre at Chinook.

MAY 30, 2000
The Telus Convention Centre opens, after doubling in cost to $70 million.

SPRING 2001
Over the past months, various stages of Chinook's $300 million renovation have opened; it's now complete.

MARCH 2001
The Famous Players Paramount Theatre opens.

OCT. 16, 2001
Dave Bronconnier becomes Calgary's 35th mayor.

DECEMBER 2002
Chinook regains position as top local mall, based on sales per square foot.

DECEMBER 2003
Visits to Chinook number 14 million for the year.

SPRING 2004
The Calgary Flames make it to Game 7 of the Stanley Cup, but lose to the Tampa Bay Lightning.

JULY 2005
Chinook's sales volume per square foot touches $700 mark, making it one of the top three malls in the country.

SPRING 2005
Flooding of the Bow and Elbow rivers leads to home evacuations and $400 million in damages.

DECEMBER 2005
Visitors spend $40 million throughout the year at Chinook's four restaurants, food court and food kiosks.

FEBRUARY 2006
Chinook plans 180,000-square-foot expansion.

DEC. 14, 2006
Ed Stelmach is sworn in as the new premier of Alberta.

SEPTEMBER 2007
The Canadian dollar achieves parity with the American buck.

APRIL 6, 2008
Calgary native Leslie Feist picks up five Junos as the city hosts the national music awards.

AUGUST 2008
Sales volume hits $905 per square foot

SEPTEMBER 2008
Calgary's red-hot economy suddenly cools, as stock markets and economies crash around the world.

NOVEMBER 2008
The Calgary Stampeders win the Grey Cup.

FALL 2009
Calgary hosts the WorldSkills Competition, an LPGA event and the Grey Cup.

WALL·E

2000s

The recipe for Chinook Centre's annual Stampede Breakfast is complex, but perfectly executed each year. Start with 1,500 kilograms of pancake batter, 1,800 kilograms of breakfast sausage and 6,000 litres of coffee. Mix in 60,000 hungry visitors, 300 volunteers, 130 flapjack flippers and dozens of entertainers. Combine all ingredients on the first Saturday of Stampede each year and the result is the city's best-known pancake breakfast.

The Chinook Centre Stampede Breakfast has become a tradition for tens of thousands of people each year and is a visible reflection of the shopping centre's involvement in community.

"It's really an unbelievable event," says local broadcast personality and real estate agent Jimmy Hughes, who emcees the event. "I was 22 the first time I was involved in the breakfast. As someone who grew up in Calgary and knew the significance of this event, this was big — really big. . . . For a broadcaster, this was something I liken to making it to the NHL. . . . It was a dream come true."

People come back to the breakfast year after year because it's exciting, explains Chris Daniels, who has handled the event's technical production for 30-plus years.

"It's a little addictive because it's so big and so intense," says Daniels, owner of Daniels Audio. "One time a year, for a few hours, tens of thousands of people come together for a great event. You put it together, it happens and then bang; it's over. It's a wonderful time."

It takes a remarkable effort by many people to make the event happen, adds Ed Harris of High Note Marketing, who has handled the breakfast's entertainment for the past decade.

2003 DOLLARS & DIGITS

Chinook Centre showed significant growth in customer numbers and spending, following renovations that ended early in the decade. By 2003, the mall was posting very successful annual numbers.

14 million: Visitors to the mall.

$650: Sales per square foot; the highest of all Calgary malls.

2.2 million: Customers at the food court.

14 million: Dollars spent at Chinook's restaurants.

12 million: Number of customers at the theatre.

MEMORABLE MOMENTS

The hands of Bryan Loschuk give pancake batter a final whisk, as Jim Patty (right) carries batter from a cement mixer manned by Joe Deiure.   *Grant Black photos*

Jim Patty, Calgary Fire Dept.:

The mixing of the flapjack batter is a key duty on the morning of the breakfast, so it's put in the hands of very trustworthy folks – firefighters. "It's an opportunity for us to do something in the community, plus we have a lot of fun," says Jim Patty, who has been creating the pancake concoction at 28 breakfasts. Patty along with colleagues – including Bryan Loschuk, Joe Deiure and Fred Deiure (who started the tradition) – use a modified cement mixer to stir the batter.

"It was a lot harder to do the mixing before we had that," says Patty. "We also used to have to add eggs in the batter, which could be interesting when you're mixing up batter for thousands and thousands of people. With the newer (eggless) batter, things go smoother."

These members of the Calgary Fire Department have their own tradition for the breakfast. They bring their spouses and kids with them, too.

"It's become a family thing for us over the years," says Patty. "It's a tradition. . . . Foreign visitors sometimes come over to get their picture taken with us. We have our regulars, too. They come by to say 'hi' every year."

Jerry Beemster:

"Stampede without the Chinook Centre Breakfast? It wouldn't be Stampede without it. People enjoy it. . . . It's what thousands of people do to enjoy Stampede every year."

Ed Harris (right), entertainment organizer for the breakfast, with sound expert Chris Daniels.

Ed Harris, entertainment organizer for the Chinook Stampede Breakfast:

"One of the talents, who graced the stage in 2001, was then 11-year-old Brett Kissel. Brett was performing at a talent show in Edmonton that I was judging.

After hearing him perform, I asked Brett if he would like to play at a breakfast in Calgary during Stampede. He promptly asked his dad if it was all right. With his dad's approval, he calmly turned to me and asked, 'How many people?' His jaw dropped when I said 20,000 or so. Brett has gone on to become a star in Canada, releasing several albums and playing to sold-out shows across the West."

Jimmy Hughes, emcee of the Stampede Breakfast:

"The Chinook Centre Breakfast probably sets the standard for events like this. It really helps spread the spirit of the Stampede across the city outside of the grounds. . . . Now, the Stampede has adopted what the Chinook Breakfast started. The Stampede has a caravan committee and it takes breakfasts to malls and locations right across the city."

Walter Klingble:

"My parents moved to the community of Fairview in 1959. When Chinook started having Stampede breakfasts here in 1960, our family started coming. . . . I remember when there was a gravel road leading to this place. I've been coming here as long as I remember."

Pat and Norm Goodberry-Dyck:

"The food is definitely fabulous, but we always come, just bring our chairs, and sit and listen to the music. . . . And, it's great to people watch."

The crowd at the Chinook Breakfast, shown here in 2009, numbers between 50,000 and 60,000 each year.

Grant Black photo

Over the years, a variety of politicians have flipped flapjacks, including Prime Minister Stephen Harper, seen here in 2007 with Ron Wratschko, a vice-president with Cadillac Fairview.

Calgary Herald Archive

"While a 7 a.m. stage call is not usually a part of an artist's routine, it has been an amazing feat that not one artist has missed the date, shown up late, or in fact complained about the early show," Harris says. Those artists — many of whom are Juno and Canadian Country Music Association award winners — include Doc Walker, Gord Bamford, George Fox, Gil Grand, The Wilkinsons, Beverley Mahood, Dick Damron and Paul Brandt.

"I think a great number of Calgarians have memories of the Chinook Breakfasts," says George Brookman, former chairman of the Calgary Stampede and owner/CEO of West Canadian Digital Imaging. Brookman himself, as a teenager employed at Woodward's, recalls how breakfast sausages in the early years were prepared in Woodward's kitchens. After thousands and thousands of sausages were cooked in the store's ovens,

Steam rises as Leslie Kitsch, one of 300 volunteers, cooks sausages for the 2009 Chinook Stampede Breakfast.

Grant Black photo

Stan Litwack:

"The Stampede wouldn't be the Stampede without this breakfast. My parents were bringing the family here since I was a kid. . . . Chinook Centre itself is a special place. This is where my mother and I used to visit all the time. We loved the Bamboo Restaurant and the Macleod Room at Woodward's before they closed. We used to come here to power walk, too, before Mom passed away." Now recently retired, Litwack visits the mall every day to meet with friends and have a morning conversation. "We talk, we tell each other jokes. We call it the boardroom," he says of the area outside Zellers where the group informally gathers. "This is our connection to life. We don't need a computer to do this. It's a place where people meet."

Oris and Ron Hanson:

After attending breakfasts for decades, sometimes in sunshine, sometimes in rain, it's easy for the couple to recall a highlight: "(Prime Minister) Stephen Harper served us our breakfast last year!"

Const. Garret Swihart:

"It's a great duty to pull. You have everyone happy and smiley, and glad to be here. You've got people from all over the world. I met some people from Australia, Israel and Michigan, so it's a lot of fun." It's a nice side of Stampede in comparison with the late night bar and club scene during the week, he says. "This is positive Stampede policing."

Gerri Lykkemark, a long-time attendee of the Chinook Breakfast, is shown here at the 2009 edition.

Gerri Lykkemark:

"I was at Chinook the day it opened and I've been coming to their Stampede Breakfast ever since. Chinook was like nothing else in Calgary. . . . Today, it's still an important part of the city. There are great stores, but you don't have to just go shopping. There's good food. You can even do yoga at Lululemon every Sunday morning. It's a great place."

Allan Andrews:

"I think that to come to the Stampede breakfast, to me, that's the start of the Stampede. . . . The breakfast itself is just wonderful. . . . and I like to watch the stage show."

Millie Serkownak:

As a former employee at Cavalier China & Gift Shop and Fairweather, Serkownak has attended almost all breakfasts. "I used to come and have breakfast; then, I watched the entertainment and then I went to work. And you know what? I used to put in 12-hour shifts."

Arthur Taylor:

This former Simpsons-Sears employee is a long-time attendee, who says, "I haven't had a bad Stampede Breakfast in all those years. . . . (However), the one thing I really regret is the year (2000) they tried for the Guinness Book of Records in serving up (the most) breakfasts (in one hour)." The Chinook Breakfast fell slightly short of the record set by Dubai, where 13,797 breakfasts were served in 60 minutes. But as Taylor points out, "All it was, was cornflakes and milk. These (Chinook) guys poured and cooked a breakfast and they still almost got it (the record.) I wrote Guinness and said that they should have a special category for an actual cooked breakfast because, hey, anybody can pour cornflakes and milk." (Chinook was indeed later given the record for hosting the biggest cooked breakfast, at the time.)

Brookman was often given the task of cleaning the stoves.

"That was my reward for being so diligent," laughs Brookman. "I'm a meticulous cleaner. I could get those ovens looking like they'd just come out of the showroom."

This kind of effort has become key to the breakfast over the years. The event wouldn't happen without the dedicated volunteers from the shopping centre, retailers, business partners and community partners, says Chinook marketing co-ordinator Alexandra Velosa, who starts planning for the breakfast in January each year.

Volunteers often enjoy the morning as much as the breakfast attendees do. The people running the grills often engage in fun competition to see who can make the best pancakes, adding toppings that range from blueberries to ice cream.

"They have a lot of fun and people enjoy it," says Velosa. "We have people who come to the breakfast every year. It is a family tradition."

The breakfast also gives Chinook the opportunity to raise money for one of its important community partners, the Alberta Children's Hospital Foundation. More than $600,000 has been given to the foundation as a result of funds collected from Chinook Centre, its merchants, business partners and friends over the years.

"We are truly grateful for the dedication of Chinook Centre, their retailers and their customers," says Saifa Koonar, the foundation's president and CEO. "Their support extends well beyond the Stampede Breakfast to include the annual Chinook golf tournament, donations from pictures with Santa, sponsoring a toy shop at our family gala and even donating flowers to brighten up the front entrance of our hospital. . . . The dedication of (Chinook manager) Terry Napper and his amazing team has had an immeasurable impact on kids and families over the years."

Chinook's work within the community extends into many arenas, including Habitat for Humanity, WinSport and the neighbouring area of Meadowlark

THE TIME CAPSULE

• Below Chinook's rotunda, a time capsule was buried six feet under the ground in 2000.
• A digital clock in the capsule's cover plate displays the current time and Chinook's position on the planet.
• The capsule is due to be opened on the eve of the next millennium, Dec. 31, 2999.
• Its contents include items representing various aspects of life in Alberta, including a white cowboy hat, newspapers, local books, a cell phone, a Starbucks coffee container, a Canadian trivia game and antibiotics.

The Egyptian-themed movie theatre at Chinook Centre, now known as Scotiabank Theatre, is one of the most successful in Canada.   *Grant Black photo*

SIGNS OF THE TIMES AT CHINOOK CENTRE

• **May 2000:** The Flames open a booth at Chinook to sell season tickets. At the time, sales had declined to such a point that the team was nearing a financial crisis; some worried that the Flames wouldn't survive in Calgary. Calgarians, however, rallied behind the team.
• **May 2001:** The Calgary Regional Health Authority sets up a kiosk at Chinook Centre to recruit nurses and give the profession increased visibility. It fills 30 of 300 available jobs from late February to early May via the booth.
• **February 2003:** The Hong Kong Economic and Trade Office wants to promote closer ties with the city, so it holds an exhibition at Chinook to display business opportunities.
• **August 2003:** Men deserve a little pampering, too, and begin heading to spas for everything from facials and massages to waxing. Diva Hair Salon and Spa in Chinook reports about 15 per cent of its spa clientele are men.
• **March 2004:** A touring photo exhibit, designed to change the way women view their bodies and to raise awareness of eating disorders, is displayed at Chinook.

When Chinook Centre completed its redevelopment in 2001, Calgarian Steve Williams — who then worked for the shopping centre's advertising agency — wrote this poem in honour of the occasion.

The Chinook Odyssey

Let us reflect,
On tribulations sent
As we consider the phenomenon
Of Chinook Centre's redevelopment.

It began with a vision,
As epic journeys often do
Amazing all concerned
By the time it was through.

"That wasn't in the blueprints"
Became a battle cry
Jonsey, aka Dr. Kevorkian
Was where invoices were sent to die.

Kilometres of hoarding
Hid a multitude of sins
Directional signage from hell
Was consigned to trash bins

"Let's go for a drink"
Was a familiar refrain
There were more hard hats than customers
And leaks during rain.

Mehak got caffeined up
And with the City he spoke
The rest of us, wisely
Bought shares in Diet Coke

And Kushar in leasing
Saw his blood pressure soar
As scaffolding went up
In front of yet another store.

Yet through all the rubble
And rebar, and dust
There was, implicitly
A feeling of trust.

Grant Black photo

Norbert kept things humming
Building stores and the like
We had no way of knowing
He needed training wheels for his bike.

The consumers, God bless them
Kept coming in for a peek
Often raising the question
"Where's Customer Service this week?"

Napper's confidence never wavered
It was all going to work
No matter how many times
He said, "I did a knee jerk."

There were naysayers, granted
But 20 Vic did it
And if something didn't work
We made sure that we hid it.

Despite the propensity
Of humans to complain
The light at the end of the tunnel
Was not a train.

Chinook Centre stands today
After three years of stress
A continent-wide achievement
And a monument to success.

The eye of the Albertosaurus glows red while guarding the entrance to Chinook.   Grant Black photo

Park. Chinook bought new playground equipment for the neighbourhood; shopping centre staff then volunteered to help install it.

"Part of our role is to be a good community partner and that can take many forms," says retail manager Paige O'Neill.

"We try to be proactive," she says, citing one example where Chinook heard about a family that did its Christmas shopping at the mall, but was robbed later that night. As a result, Chinook sent the family a generous gift card to use at the shopping centre.

"It's about being aware of your community and what's happening," says O'Neill.

As Chinook moved into the new millennium, work progressed on the massive renovation started in 1998. Chinook was spending $210 million on the revamp, while retailers were investing an additional $100 million in their own stores.

A significant addition to the plan was announced in early 2000. City hall gave approval for construction of a massive Egyptian-themed Famous Players project that would include 4,000 seats in 16 theatres and an Imax auditorium.

Different phases of the renovation opened at various times, but the entire revamp was complete in the spring of 2001. It marked the end of one of the most comprehensive mall redevelopments in Canada's retail history. Highlights included $750,000 in public art installations, such as the moving airplane sculptures above the food court and a replica of an Albertosaurus.

The Albertosaurus, standing seven metres tall and weighing three tonnes, was built of oilrig pieces, farm machinery and auto parts. Part of a 1932 Dodge pick-up's hood was used for the sculpture's head. A smudge pot formed the heart. Bucket arms from front-end loaders were used for the legs. And the vertebrae came from a grain elevator chain and pulleys from threshing machines.

"It's a reminder of this area, of the land and what stood on it and passed over it," artist Russell Zeid said at the time. "The Albertosaurus roamed the grounds of Chinook 75 million years ago, and 75 years ago most of the parts of the dino were roaming around the field here as farm machinery. It is symbolic and it's fun."

Once the revamped shopping centre was unveiled, Calgarians were delighted to see the new look of the mall. Natural light poured into the shopping centre. Dozens of comfortable seating areas

MEMORABLE MOMENTS

Grant Black photo

Eddie Wong, owner of the Arby's franchise: "The food court has been a very good place to own a business. . . . The best decision I made in my life was to marry my wife (Esther.) The second best decision I made was to have an Arby's franchise."

Calgary Herald Archive

Dave Bronconnier, Calgary mayor, elected 2001: "I grew up in Calgary, so I remember going to Chinook as a kid, for everything from the Stampede Breakfast to the movies. . . . We used to go for the malts and the Orange Julius drinks, too," says Bronconnier. "Chinook Centre is like Calgary in that they've both grown up together. Chinook is more than a retail experience; it's a great people place. It's a great spot."

Tom Donaldson, owner of Chinook's Edo Japan franchise: "Chinook is everybody's mall. People visit the mall that is closest to them and most convenient. And, most people also visit Chinook. It means everybody in Calgary has two malls and one of them is Chinook. Everybody knows Chinook. There are very few malls like it."

Natural light, greenery and plenty of seating greet customers at the Food Court.

MEMORABLE MOMENTS

Sheldon (Yogi) Bartlett, mechanical supervisor for Chinook:

"A lot of mechanical things need to happen to make this building run . . . but what makes the building is the people. The people are special. . . . You can find everything you need here, too. . . . My doctor is here, my dentist is here. I could likely survive in this building without going outside."

Jody Reid, senior manager, Security & Life Safety at Chinook:

"Back during the renovations around 1998 I was working the graveyard shift (overnight) alone. The mall was very dark as there was minimal lighting during the construction at night. . . . Lots of exterior walls were missing and there were lots of scary noises! I was out on patrol in the north end one night and I could see something just bigger than a cat waddling down the mall toward me. I pulled out my trusty Mini-Mag light and was able to illuminate the area in front of me. It was a muskrat waddling down the common area. I sprung into action. I screamed at it and waved my arms in an effort to scare off the beast. It hissed at me, showed me its fangs and started waddling very quickly toward me. This is not what was supposed to happen. I ran very fast in the opposite direction

and was able to flee to safety on the upper level. I never saw that evil creature again. I also carried a bigger flashlight on nights after that."

Robert Nowak, Chinook's Assistant Operations Manager:

After 20-plus years in the shopping centre industry, Nowak has become known for his practical jokes. However, his favourite memory focuses on former staff. "We had our own cleaning staff . . . with about 25 employees (many whom were born outside of Canada). We introduced a program with Alberta Vocational College for learning English at work. About 20 employees studied hard, mostly after hours on their own time for about a year. So, as we were coming to that moment, Graduation Day, we booked Casey's for lunch, and invited the teachers from AVC to present diplomas to our staff. They all showed up wearing suits, tuxedos, Sunday get-ups. . . . It was like they were graduating university. . . . and it made my day."

Peggy Lim, Chinook Centre Marketing Director:

"When I was younger, my dad would drive me to Chinook every Boxing Day (my birthday). We'd arrive right as the stores opened and we shopped (for my birthday gift, of course, and to spend my Christmas cash from grandparents),

and shopped and shopped. My dad would eventually leave my mom and me to continue shopping and he'd wait in the car. Who would have thought I'd be part of the Chinook family and be at the centre even earlier now (before stores open) on Boxing Day to help out, observe and people watch." Lim also recalls a more recent favourite moment when the centre's leasing manager was showing the mall to representatives from Tiffany & Co. "We had 25 models dressed as Audrey Hepburn and George Peppard (from the movie Breakfast at Tiffany's), roaming through the mall as if they were shopping. Seeing customers' reactions and having customers stop the models to take photos with them was priceless."

Dennis McGowean, Operations Manager at Chinook Centre:

Special events including the Charity Bazaar and Stampede Breakfasts stand out as highlights of McGowean's quarter century in the shopping centre business. "It was a lot different than these days, as we (myself, my operations supervisor and the six maintenance staff) set everything up, including the stage, and had to complete it in one day. By the end of the teardown you were too tired to do anything else but sleep."

were scattered throughout. An obvious central court area and improved walkways made navigation straightforward. Of the 220 merchants, 213 completely redesigned or built new stores. The calibre of shops and food outlets, as well as the interior and exterior of the building, drew praise.

"Retailers have emerged from the imposed discipline of the faceless mall exterior with their own unique identities, and their own direct access into the building," local architect Peter Burgener of BKDI wrote at the time in a Calgary Herald column. "The result is a much more dynamic, visually interesting structure."

On the inside, "a low key, pleasantly lighted space, with nicely detailed finishes and a simple, comprehensible organization plan are offered," said Burgener. "And the part that most clearly reflects the whole new attitude is the comfortable seating generously positioned throughout the centre. . . . (A) gracious and human approach also forms the basis of the 'wow!' space — the central food court. There are lots of lights, more comfortable seating and a great interior volume of space that feels good to be in."

Living through the renovations was challenging for some, but it also presented business opportunities, says Arby's franchisee Eddie Wong. Wong agreed to be one of the last "old" food kiosks to stay open, while the transition was made to the new court in a renovated area of the mall.

"By staying open, my business tripled," says Wong, who was a teacher in Hong Kong before arriving in Canada. Business has thrived in his location in the new food court, too. Wong's franchise has been Arby's best performer, in terms of volume of sales in the food court category.

The reasons for his success are simple. He keeps food quality high for the 400 to 600 customers served each day, and he enjoys the job he's doing. Staff retention and morale are also key, he says.

"I give them recognition and treat them with respect," Wong says. Some employees have been with Wong for a decade, which is significant in the fast food industry.

It's a good place to work, says employee Irene Lee. "He makes it a happy place for staff."

The comment is music to Wong's ears. "On the first day the food court opened,

INNOVATIONS & INVENTIONS OF THE 21ST CENTURY:

- **2001:** The iPod, a fuel cell bike, Wikipedia and Windows XP are unveiled.
- **2002:** Europe adopts the Euro as its official currency; breath strips hit the market.
- **2003:** iTunes is launched; 150,000 hybrid cars are sold by Toyota; the Human Genome Project is completed; the first cloned horse is created.
- **2004:** More than $1.6 billion is raised in the first public stock offering of Google.
- **2005:** YouTube is invented; the Xbox 360 gaming system is put on shelves.
- **2006:** Pluto is no longer a full-fledged planet and becomes a "dwarf planet"; Nintendo's Wii is introduced.
- **2007:** The iPhone becomes available; a battery that runs on sugar is invented; Google Maps begin offering Street View.
- **2008:** Twitter rises to fame; ice is found on Mars, meaning the planet has water; a successful bionic hand is created.
- **2009:** The World Digital Library is launched by UNESCO.

Grant Black photos

BY THE NUMBERS:

- **1,400:** Children who visited Santa at Chinook on the busiest holiday shopping day in 2000.
- **480:** Chairs and couches in the shopping centre, once the renovation was completed in 2000.
- **1.2 million:** Square footage of space in Chinook Centre after renovations were finished.
- **10.96 billion:** Dollars that Calgarians spent on retail goods and services in 2000, a 10 per cent increase from 1999.
- **3:** Extra hours Chinook decided to open each Saturday evening to make Saturday night shopping a year-round offering.
- **300:** Wannabe models that turned up at the Famous Players Paramount Theatre to compete in the first Famous Face of Calgary model search in 2002.
- **40,000:** Average number of daily shoppers at Chinook Centre.
- **47,000:** People who visited the mall Jan. 1, 2003, the first New Year's Day that a major mall opened for business in Calgary.
- **90,000:** People who shopped at Chinook Centre on Boxing Day in 2002.
- **409.5:** The number of hours Chinook was open for holiday shopping from Nov. 25 to Jan 1, 2007.

Monica Zurowski photo

The food court has become one of Canada's best, in terms of sales and quality.   *Monica Zurowski photo*

I told myself, 'Eddie, you made a good decision.' . . . There were many customers; and, people loved this place."

Many outlets throughout the food court quickly declared the area a success and enjoyed a boom in business. Edo Japan, for example, became a top performer.

"People want to eat something that tastes better," explains franchise owner Tom Donaldson. "Edo's food is hot, fresh and good; it's comfort food."

The entire food court quickly garnered rave reviews, even prompting some customers to tip the staff cleaning tables. The area became a highlight of the reno and eventually became one of the highest grossing food courts in Canada.

"I think it's one of the best food courts I've ever seen," says Hart Abercrombie, one of the original owners of the Stephen Avenue Soup Co. and local New York Fries franchises. "The food court is great. It's interesting. The seating area is interesting. . . . Even though it's now 10 years old, it's still one of the top food courts in Western Canada."

The area oozes comfort, says retail manager Paige O'Neill. "When I walk through the food court with the big trees and the windows, it's like a breath of fresh air."

The renovations outside the food court also attracted attention, winning customer and retailer acclaim.

"I remember the first time I saw our store in Chinook," says Karen Flavelle, president of Purdy's Chocolates. "It was a tiny little thing on the outside of the Bay, and Chinook was broken into two parts. I think we moved seven times as the mall was renovated." The staff, however, did an excellent job of being flexible as changes occurred and the reno results were wonderful, she says.

Chinook's stores have always offered an interesting array of merchandise, but more than that, the mall presents a pleasurable experience for families, says former fashion writer Joanne Good.

"It's one of the most efficient places to cope with winter. . . . Plus, it's a quintessential marketplace because it meets the needs of everyone, whatever their age," she says. Teens can explore and experience a bit of freedom, while their parents do the shopping and their grandparents get some exercise by walking around the mall. "It makes for a successful outing for the entire family," she says.

The success of the renovation was also quickly reflected in retail figures. Sales in the mall in August 2000 were 105 per cent higher than the previous August.

By March 2002, even more favourable figures were recorded. More than one million people a month were visiting Chinook. The sales volume of non-anchor stores was $260 million, the highest of any Calgary mall. Those sales were predicted to reach $300 million that year, doubling the centre's 1997 total, which had been the most successful year to date.

"We always had a dream that we could do $300 million, but in all honesty, it was a dream," centre manager Terry Napper told the Herald at the time. "The sales volumes have exceeded our expectations."

The food court, meanwhile, was serving more than two million people a year, with sales in excess of $14 million. People were also flocking to the Famous Players Paramount Theatre. Customers loved the theatre's special features, which included innovative sound systems, plush chairs, full-width floor-to-ceiling screens and a steeply sloped floor, meaning customers could see over the head of the person in front of them.

Later that year, Chinook also reclaimed a ranking it had lost to Market Mall. It became the Calgary mall with the highest sales volume per square foot of space, in non-anchor stores, over a 12-month period. This important industry standard put Chinook at $605 per square foot, followed by Market Mall at $575.

Big-name stores continued to make a home in Chinook, giving shoppers even more reason to head to the mall. L'Occitane opened in 2000; Old Navy in 2002; and, Williams-Sonoma and Pottery Barn in 2005. American chain stores prospered, partly due to familiarity. There are a significant number of American citizens who live in the city and many Calgarians frequently travel to the U.S.

The Cadillac Fairview Corporation Limited

Peter Sharpe, President and CEO Cadillac Fairview:

"Chinook is one of the most productive shopping centres in the entire country, delivering among the highest sales per square foot in the industry. Led by an experienced team and offering a dynamic retail mix, it has grown in popularity to become one of Canada's busiest shopping centres as well."

Alexandra Velosa, Chinook Centre marketing co-ordinator:

Velosa and husband Carlos Herrera moved from Colombia in November 2003, in search of improved opportunities for their then four-year-old son Nicolas. Money was tight, so the couple explained there wouldn't be many Christmas gifts, as Santa didn't know where they lived yet. Nicolas wrote Santa a letter explaining the situation, and noting he'd left all his toys behind for poor children. The family went to Chinook to visit Santa and Nicolas delivered the letter. A few days later, a stranger came to the door, Velosa recalls. "He explained he was a friend of Santa's and Santa had asked him to drop something off. . . . He gave us bags and bags of toys and books and treats. It was wonderful." Several years later when Velosa became a Chinook employee, she tried to find out who was behind this act of kindness, but no one had the answer. "We don't know who did it, but we know it was very, very special."

Calgary Herald Archive

Ken King, President and CEO Calgary Flames

"Calgary is fortunate to have more than its share of icons – people, architecture, rodeo, festivals and even home sports teams. Iconic, too, is our landmark Chinook Shopping Centre, historically relevant and a retail smash hit."

---

this change is good," Tait continues. "I always look at retail as entertainment. . . . Whether you spend your money on movies or hockey or shopping, that's entertainment. The renovations here make this form of entertainment much more positive. There are 80 new stores. That's good for shoppers and that's good for retailers. We're excited about it."

The expansion is injecting enthusiasm into the north end of the mall, says M-C Green, Sears manager. "It's something we're looking forward to seeing."

The changes will be a bonus for customers, some of whom have been long-term patrons, and for businesses themselves, adds Glenda Tetreau, owner of Merle Norman Cosmetics and Day Spa at Chinook. "We're the best kept secret in Canada, in terms of quality and value of products. . . . Increased traffic in the mall helps us build on a loyal customer base."

Chinook Centre has undergone incredible transformation over the years, says Andrea Stephen, executive vice-president of investments for Cadillac Fairview.

"Chinook is a flagship asset," says Stephen. "The sales per square foot are impressive. We've had enquiries about whether we would sell. . . . But it's a core asset for us. It represents what we are trying to accomplish in terms of brand, and that is the 'best.' We want the best; we want quality in investments."

The focus on quality, along with the mall's location, contributes to its success and makes it a milestone in Calgary, O'Neill adds. "Out-of-towners use it as a landmark when they're figuring out where they are in the city. . . . And for Calgarians, it's a marker on Macleod Trail. When someone says something is on Macleod Trail, they often will add whether it's north or south of Chinook."

Chinook is both a "tourist mall and a local mall," says Lucy Thibault, district manager for Purdy's. "I know there are many people who visit the city and choose Chinook as the place to shop. And, there are the locals who have been coming here for years; they are people who are very committed to Chinook."

Fran Clarke, manager and co-owner of the Chinook Bowladrome, sits on one of the original benches outside the basement bowling centre.   Grant Black photo

It's interesting to note Chinook "started on the fringe of the city; but it is now almost in the centre of Calgary," says Barry Styles, former CEO of the Highwood Communications agency that handled the centre's advertising. "Chinook is very much in the middle of things."

The shopping centre has also become an important part of people's lives in other ways. For some, it's the place where they've met other people — meetings that have blossomed into friendships, relationships and even love.

"I worked with my husband's mother at Woodward's and that's how I met him," explains Lois Fischer. "Jim would come in to visit his mother at work from time to time. . . . It wasn't love at first sight, but it was love at about fifth sight."

For Paige O'Neill herself, she met her husband — radio personality Matt O'Neill — at an event Chinook hosted for media. Matt then invited Paige for an interview on his Jack FM radio show to talk about the upcoming Stampede Breakfast. He later queried if she was single (she was),

Jessica Polivchuk 'glow' bowls at the Chinook Bowladrome, which was one of the shopping centre's first features when it opened 50 years ago.   *Grant Black photo*

and she then invited him to the breakfast. "We count the breakfast at Chinook as our first date," she says.

"Chinook Centre really has its own culture," adds Sheldon (Yogi) Bartlett, the mall's mechanical supervisor. "I met my wife (Denise Bazzana, now Bartlett) here. She was a manager at Roots and I got a phone call. . . . There was an air conditioning unit at the store that sounded like a helicopter taking off."

The fan belt had split and the conversation over repairs was the first time the two talked. Romance bloomed, followed by marriage. The couple now shares a special Christmas ritual. They wake up at 6 a.m. and head to Chinook to complete Bartlett's daily "walk through" to ensure everything is operating as it should.

That sense of connectedness to Chinook is also seen through a multi-generational aspect, as children and even grandchildren of original employees make their way in the world at the shopping centre.

"It's wonderful to see the next generation be inspired by their parents," says Don McGregor, who has employed children of former employees at his successful Orange Julius stands. McGregor himself is part of this generational trend, since his father Ken was the first mall manager.

Those family roots are seen at other places, too. Two of Phil Streifel's sons now run his Chinook Barber Shop. Next door at Chinook Optical, Biba Tharp has become owner and taken over the store built by her father.

There is something special about following in your father's footsteps, says Tharp, noting her dad originally created the store with the idea that her grandfather would run it.

Tharp's route to Chinook, however, wasn't a direct one. She travelled through Europe; working, studying and becoming involved in design, before finding her way back to Chinook Optical. "It's a people job," she says. "I love it."

Chinook Centre manages to stay relevant to generation after generation, notes Eve Renaud, who is the centre's assistant general manager and daughter of Ron Renaud, mall manager in the late 1970s.

"Chinook has changed over time, but it always remembers its roots and the things that are important, such as community and people," she says.

The history of Chinook does make it a special place, says Fran Clarke, general manager of the Chinook Bowladrome, which has been open since day one.

"There's nostalgia here," says Clarke. Visitors can check out bowling shoes, balls, and even fibreglass seats from 50 years ago. Some of the original flooring from the mall is also still visible outside the alley's doors.

"Back in the '50s, that's when bowling really took off," says Clarke, herself a former champion bowler. "Entire families would bowl. . . . It was something that many families came to Chinook to do."

For many, that tradition continues today. Jessica Polivchuk's entire family has participated in the sport at the Bowladrome over the years, with various family members winning bowling awards. "I love it here," says Polivchuck, a Bowladrome employee and youth coach. "It's full of great people."

The immediate future of Chinook includes an 80-store expansion on the northeast side of the centre, as shown in these renderings. Artwork courtesy Cadillac Fairview

The Future

To make the magic of a mall happen, a team of dedicated, professional individuals and business partners works tirelessly behind the scenes to ensure smooth operation of the multimillion-dollar asset, Chinook Centre. A number of areas — including operations, accounting, security, marketing, administration, customer service and leasing — comes together with a single goal.

"The goal is to lead the shopping centre industry in continually raising guests' expectations about what shopping should be — fun, comfortable, safe and stimulating," says communications manager Stacie Woolford.

That means attention is paid to every detail. Security personnel must be visible and accessible. The mall is kept clean and comfortable. Promotions run flawlessly, stores are unique and a friendly greeting is always available at the Customer Service Centre.

"It's all about our guests," says Shannon Perschon, specialty leasing representative. Dozens and dozens of people come together in a myriad of different ways to make sure the Chinook Centre experience is the best one possible.

At the heart of the building is the 24-hour security and operations centre, a communications hub assigned the task of ensuring all systems are running efficiently. Cooling units and heating systems work round the clock to keep the shopping centre's temperature regulated. Hundreds of miles of pipes snake through ceilings, floors and walls to move water, gas and electrical wiring throughout the centre. Fourteen electrical rooms ensure power is directed where it needs to go. The central communication centre allows staff to monitor all these operations and make changes, via a sophisticated computer system.

DEPARTMENT STORES

Then: Twenty-five years ago, Chinook's anchor department stores — Woodward's and Simpsons-Sears — comprised the bulk (60 per cent) of Chinook's sales; $120 million of the mall's $200 million total annual sales.

Now: The current anchor stores — Sears, The Bay and Zellers — account for less than $80 million of the shopping centre's $550 million annual sales, or 15 per cent.

Next: Specialty shops will continue to grow in popularity, while department stores work to maintain or grow their current levels of sales.

SHOPPING HOURS

Then: Fifty years ago, stay-at-home mothers did the bulk of the shopping Tuesday to Friday between 9 a.m. and 5 p.m.

Now: Shopping is usually a shared duty in families, often completed on weeknights and weekends.

Next: Retailers will continue to examine hours of operation to accommodate the changing needs of society.

PARKING

Then: Fifty years ago, there were 3,000 to 3,500 parking stalls at Chinook.

Now: More than 5,500 stalls, including 1,200 underground heated spots, will be available by fall 2010.

Next: Potential future development includes short-term parking designations, cell phone waiting areas (where drivers wait until the person they're picking up calls to indicate he or she is ready to leave the mall), and valet parking in some areas of the centre.

Parking, as shown in this mid-1990s photo, has changed and grown at the mall over the past half-century. Calgary Herald Archive

The mechanical rooms, which are home to Chinook Centre's major heating and cooling units, are light, bright and clean, much like the centre itself. Grant Black photo

"Many parts of the mall don't need heat most days, due to the ambient heat generated in here," says mechanical supervisor Sheldon (Yogi) Bartlett, adding that the centre becomes more energy efficient every year. "But we're here to make any adjustments that are required."

Bartlett and team walk the one-kilometre stretch of mall many times each week, through a maze of hidden hallways, passageways and tunnels. "The back of the house is complex," says Bartlett. "Most people could get lost here."

That's quite true, agrees former marketing director Bev Blue, who recalls she and other Chinook staff spent time exploring some far reaches of the basement in the 1990s. "We found a room that had been neglected for decades," Blue says. "Inside, we found boxes and boxes and boxes of cash register tape from the Chinook Drive-In," which sat on the site decades earlier.

The basement stretches under much of the south end of Chinook, providing thousands of square feet of storage space. As part of the centre's future plans, construction is currently ongoing to optimize the basement space.

"We will have over 120 storage locations and we need them," says centre manager Terry Napper. "Look at a place like Pottery Barn. They have an 8,000-square-foot store and they need almost the same amount of storage space because of their larger items. . . . Without storage, there wouldn't be a Pottery Barn at Chinook.

"Overall, it's a very complicated building," says Napper. "There are 19 different ways to get into this building and eight different ways onto the site."

The shopping centre is also moving closer to a 24-hour-a-day operation. By the time theatre staff leave after the late movies end, it's almost 2 a.m. and em-

Terry Napper, manager of Chinook Centre, says the current expansion will help the shopping centre accommodate future retail trends.

CHINOOK CENTRE EXPANSION

- 1.2 million construction man hours to complete the project;
- 14,933 truckloads of dirt to be removed from the excavation site — equivalent to 90 Olympic-size swimming pools;
- Roughly 500 tonnes of structural steel to be used;
- 10 Olympic-size swimming pools would be required to hold the amount of concrete used in the project, a total of 3,000 large cement trucks;
- The total expansion site area (390,000 square feet) is equivalent to 78 typical house lots.

Source: Chinook Centre

Terry Napper, general manager of Chinook Centre, says Calgary's retail community is eager to secure a spot in the expanding shopping centre.

Leah Hennel, Calgary Herald

Calgary retail sales to mushroom

Projection welcome news as Chinook Centre grows

MARIO TONEGUZZI
CALGARY HERALD

Retail sales in Calgary will balloon to $29.3 billion a year by 2012 — about a $6.5-billion increase from this year, according to the Conference Board of Canada.

The continued impressive annual growth in the city's retail sector falls in the same timeline as the completion of

Chinook Centre's massive redevelopment plans.

The Conference Board in its Metropolitan Outlook Autumn 2008 says Calgary is forecast to see retail sales of $22.8 billion this year, a 4.2 per cent increase from 2007. But in each of the next four years, annual growth will be over six per cent.

"Seeing as Calgary's economy continues to create jobs, personal income growth is again poised to build on previous years' impressive results," says the Conference Board. "This will provide consumers with plenty of additional money to spend, which is why the Conference Board expects retail sales growth to come in at 4.2 per cent this year on the heels of a seven per cent rise in 2007."

Those numbers are buoyed by expected strong income growth in the city. The Conference Board says personal income per capita will rise in Calgary from $53,961 this year to $60,805 in 2012. As a comparison, personal income per capita in Canada will grow from $36,947 in 2008 to $41,846 in 2012.

The Calgary forecast is good news for Chinook Centre as it proceeds at full speed with its $275-million expansion, which will bring dozens of new international retailers to the Calgary mall.

On Wednesday, Terry Napper, general manager of Chinook Centre, offered an update on the massive project, saying "the strength of this building is it's been touted as being so

CALGARY ECONOMIC INDICATORS

	Personal income per capita	Retail Sales
2005	$45,445	$17.6 billion
2006	$50,177	$20.4 billion
2007	$52,201	$21.9 billion
2008 F	$53,961	$22.8 billion
2009 F	$55,597	$24.3 billion
2010 F	$57,189	$25.9 billion
2011 F	$58,920	$27.5 billion
2012 F	$60,805	$29.3 billion

F = Forecast
Source: The Conference Board of Canada

successful that there's still a tremendous amount of interest from the retail community in getting a location here."

The expansion will add 180,000 square feet to the existing mall, two levels of

heated underground parking with 1,200 stalls, and 80 new stores, of which more than 30 are global brands not currently in the Calgary area.

SEE CHINOOK, PAGE D7

---

ployees at retail stores are arriving at the mall to stock shelves and racks.

"It's the mall that never sleeps," says Napper.

Understanding the behind-the-scene operations of Chinook is key to understanding its future. That's because for every step forward that Chinook takes, there are dozens of people preparing the way to ensure that step is successful.

The immediate future includes Chinook's current expansion, scheduled for completion in fall 2010. Additions include 180,000 square feet of new space, a two-level heated underground parking

structure and 80 new stores.

The metamorphosis — overseen by PCL Construction — began with the digging of a huge hole for the parking, on the northeast side of the mall near Macleod Trail. From that point onwards, hundreds of different tradesmen and construction workers laboured, doing everything from rebar and concrete pours to pipe installation and dry walling.

There are a huge number of pieces to keep track of at various times, says George Lineham, assistant superintendent for the job site. "I call it a chess game," he says.

The expansion is needed to ensure Chi-

nook can adapt in the future, says Bob Bertram, executive vice-president of investments for the Ontario Teachers Pension Plan, owners of Cadillac Fairview.

"I think the mall business has evolved over time," says Bertram. "Going back in Chinook's history, Woodward's was by far the dominant store in the mall, and some of that was based on hardware and furniture sales. Most people go elsewhere for those kinds of goods now. Those items have gone out of malls, into big boxes and power centres, so shopping centres need to keep changing with the times.

"You have to keep reinvesting in malls to keep them relevant," Bertram says.

Future trends for shopping centres include continued growth when it comes to the purchasing power of teens and the opening of a greater number of American stores, such as Bath & Body Works, pictured here.

Monica Zurowski photo

"You need to keep them a compelling marketplace for the consumers."

The Chinook expansion is crucial for several reasons, agrees Napper.

"Once and for all, it should eliminate the perception that Chinook doesn't have enough parking," he says. Stalls will number more than 5,500, including 1,200 heated underground spots.

"There is enough parking for this building 95 per cent of the time," Napper continues. "You could never build enough parking to handle the volume of traffic here on Boxing Day. . . but that's the case everywhere else on Boxing Day, too."

Secondly, the addition will ensure Chinook has the amount of space it needs, so that it can respond to retail trends. "What is hot today will not be hot 10 years from now," says Napper. "Consumers will change and that will mean things need to change here, too. The

worst thing that can happen to a building is no change," he says. "There shouldn't be a day that goes by when a new store isn't under construction."

Retailers agree that the ongoing expansion is vital to keep fresh blood pumping through the veins of Chinook.

"It's very cool that Chinook is 50 years old, but it hasn't stayed stagnant," says John Tait, owner of the Discovery Hut. "It's grown and it's progressed. . . . They (Chinook management) understand retail extremely well and they want to do whatever they can to make this retail experience the best. . . . That means growth."

The evolution of Chinook Centre and its future development provide an interesting story, says David Parker, an economic developer and a business columnist.

"Calgary has experienced huge developments in the retail sector both in suburban strip centres, re-merchandising of existing malls and development of new big box centres," says Parker.

"But Chinook Centre continues to be the destination choice for its faithful band of shoppers and high-end, brand merchants will attract many more. . . . No doubt, more stores and services will be added to keep it ahead of its competitors, and to keep the returns for its retailers at the top of the Calgary scale."

Chinook is indeed maintaining its status as the dominant shopping centre in Calgary, says Dave Miner, a principal at Cohos Evamy and project architect. "When Calgary hit its last little boom, it attracted the attention of American retailers who saw Calgary as a profitable place to do business. . . . I think we will see more of them in the future."

THEN, NOW AND NEXT: SECURITY

Grant Black photo

Then: Fifteen years ago, Chinook spent $200,000 annually on security.
Now: The cost in 2009 is about $2.5 million for the year.
Next: Security staff numbers and costs will continue to rise. "Security is the fastest growing expenditure the building has," says Chinook Centre manager Terry Napper. "It is an area that is vital to shopping centres for the benefit of consumers."

As new shops open, Chinook has transitioned from being a Calgary-centric property to being much more international, featuring high-end brands, says Darryl Schmidt, director of leasing in Calgary for Cadillac Fairview. "We're positioning this asset to compete with the best shopping centres in the world. We have a growing number of brands that will now have their own stores, where consumers get full exposure to the brand. . . . People will see the entire breadth of these collections. . . . With this expansion, we're just seeing the tip of the iceberg," he says, noting there will be future waves of high-end branded stores.

At the same time, local entrepreneurs will still have a vital role at the centre, often through franchise operations. Outstanding franchisees are visible in the food court, for example, notes Napper.

"We have some of the best operators in the fast food business," he says. "You see local business people in the food court. You see great entrepreneurs."

Other future growth means that down the road, the building and its retailers will continue to change with consumers' preferences and desires, says Napper.

"Just look at the change in fashion retailers. Fifteen years ago, there were clear divisions. Stores either sold menswear or women's clothes. There was a very small unisex market. Today if you look at fashion shops, most of it is unisex."

The ballooning teen market will also continue to impact the shopping centre. By evolving, the centre has been able to stay meaningful to generation after generation, says Mike Mehak, whose work with Chinook has taken on several roles over 30-plus years, including project manager of the last redevelopment. "It will continue to be a place where the next generation of kids will think of it as their mall."

"Teens have become big consumers," agrees Napper. "Baby boomers have plateaued. Baby boomers have their homes, furniture, cars. . . . There probably isn't one of them who couldn't go in their closet and live off the clothes they already have," says Napper.

"We have to figure out what they need and want, and take care of them, while taking care of the teenage market, too." Addressing the needs of the more mature customer could lead to a surge of

The new expansion on the northeast side of the shopping centre, shown here in summer 2009, will enable Chinook to keep pace with world-renowned malls.

Grant Black photo

health, nutrition, vitamin and lifestyle stores, while still maintaining a mix that ensures stores exist for all age groups.

The mix of retailers is important, adds Schmidt, noting the current expansion will allow Chinook to have more offerings at a slightly higher price point.

To complement these stores, the expansion will feature simple yet sophisticated finishings. "It will feel very much like a high-end hotel lobby, with natural materials, warmth and great light," says Miner, noting highlights will include a grand court area and crystal chandelier. "I think it will be spectacular."

Great growth potential exists for Chinook, as the Calgary market matures, says Peter Sharpe, president and CEO of Cadillac Fairview. "We are in the midst of a major . . . expansion that will be completed in 2010. Cadillac Fairview is confident that this will further enhance the shopper experience, offering consumers an even greater selection of high quality stores and 1,200 additional parking spots," he says.

The centre will house 260 retailers, plus department stores, by 2011. Eighty brand new stores will have opened and 100 existing retailers will have renovated, moved, grown or left. Every year after that, an average of five to 10 per cent of stores will be in transition.

The building will continue to work towards becoming greener. By 2014 or 2015, a major redevelopment of the food court is likely, followed by significant renovation on the north end of the mall.

Growth will also occur on the east side of Macleod Trail, Napper says, and by 2020, expect residential development to occur. "More people will want to live, work, shop and dine within a smaller area. . . . You'll see more young, urban couples with one car, so they'll want to be able to walk to work. And boomers will be selling their houses . . . and looking for convenient areas where they can relocate. Eventually, Chinook will become a true urban centre."

With residential development comes new public amenities, says Napper,

Future changes at Chinook Centre will be focused on, and built around, the changing needs and desires of its customer base.

Calgary Herald Archive

which could mean anything from an arts facility to recreational components, such as a skating rink. Canadians are already seeing this type of retail evolution. An example is the Shops at Don Mills — a recently redeveloped Cadillac Fairview property being called "Ontario's first urban village," showcasing stores, restaurants, public spaces and amenities.

"(Retail manager) Paige (O'Neill) and I talk about how when Chinook was built, it was built by the community; it was built by Calgarians," says Napper. "Now, that could be part of the future. Let the community tell us what they want and need. Chinook has always been close to the community and supported it; you need to do that if you want the community to support you."

Chinook's future could even include a hotel, says Napper. There's already a substantial base, since there can be 80 or so out-of-town salespeople and retail head office staff in the mall daily.

"Twenty years from now, we'll have hotels, office towers and condominiums," Napper predicts.

When Chinook Centre was first unveiled to the public, it was presented as a city within a city and was home to everything from doctors' and insurance offices to florists and a bowling alley.

Today, with its continued development, that phrase rings even more true. For those who were part of Chinook's opening 50 years ago, the growth makes sense.

"I love the mall today," says Amy Jennings, daughter-in-law of Reg Jennings, one of Chinook's founders.

"It's so comfortable. There's a great variety of shops and restaurants. . . . Times have changed and the shopping centre has changed with them."

Reg Jennings and partner Red Dutton would also likely be pleased to see how the shopping centre they created has grown up, right alongside the city of Calgary, say family and friends.

"Mr. Dutton always said this was going to be the centre of Calgary someday," says Boots Rogers, one of the original merchants in the mall. "He was right."

PREDICTED FUTURE TRENDS FOR RETAIL

- **Shopping for a greener world:** People will continue to seek out goods that are produced with minimal impact on the environment.
- **Viva value:** The financial challenges of 2008/09 reminded many people that they want good value when spending their retail dollars. Disposable or overly trendy items have become less desirable.
- **Shopping as a social experience:** With an increasing number of goods being available through online shopping, people want their mall experiences to be pleasurable, social and all-inclusive, often encompassing dining and entertainment aspects.
- **Tapping into technology:** A growing number of retailers will use social media such as Facebook and Twitter to communicate with customers, often inviting them to personalized shopping events. Notices of sales and special offers will be sent to mobile devices such as Blackberries, with electronic coupons and gift certificates replacing their paper equivalents.

ACKNOWLEDGEMENTS

Thanks to the following organizations and individuals for sharing their photographs, stories, research and memories:

The Calgary Herald • Glenbow Archives • Calgary Public Library timelines • Calgary Municipal Handbooks • Canadian Encyclopedia • Infoplease.com • Meadowlark Park Community Association • Canwest Archives • Suburban Modern-Postwar Dreams in Calgary by Robert M. Stamp • The Developers by James Lorimer • driveintheater.com/history/ • Chinook Bowladrome • thepeoplehistory.com • Consumer Association of Canada • Statistics Canada

Hart Abercrombie • Allan Andrews • Sheldon (Yogi) Bartlett • Jerry Beemster • Eloise Berry • Bob Bertram • Bev Blue • Stan Boniferro • Lorne Braithwaite • Paul Brandt • Phil Brien • George Brookman • Dave Bronconnier • Maureen Carol • Joe Clark • Fran Clarke • Jim Conklin • Carmine D'Ambola • Chris Daniels • Peter de Graaf • Rita de Graaf • Jim Dinning • Jack Donahue • Tom Donaldson • Barry Erskine • Patti Falconer • Julie Ferguson • Pam Fieber • Verne Fielder • Lois Fischer • Karen Flavelle • Betty Flock • John Forzani • Jean Franklyn • Joanne Good • Norm Goodberry-Dyck • Pat Goodberry-Dyck • M-C Green • Jim Hannan • Keith Hannan • Ron Hanson • Oris Hanson • Laureen Harper • Al Hardstaff • Ed Harris • Dan Hays • Helga Hilbert • Marv Holman • Joanna Howard • Jimmy Hughes • Roger Jarvis • Amy Jennings • Roy Jennings • Maureen Karran • John Kennedy • Lois Kimball • Ken King • Walter Klingble • Ralph Klein • Murray Knechtel • Bob Knight • Saifa Koonar • Trudy Kung • Barry Lammle • Irene Lee • Jean Leslie • Peggy Lim • George Lineham • Stan Litwack • Henry Liebelt • Cindy Liebelt • Mac Logan • Jackie Long • Jon Love • Gerri Lykkemark • Carolyn Matiisen • Jeff MacKinnon • Megan McCarthy • Ken McCowan • Shelley McCullough • Dennis McGowean • Don McGregor • Mike Mehak • Ron Meiers • Dave Miner • Robert Mitchell • Doreen Morgan • Karen Mottishaw • Terry Napper • Robert Nowak • Paige O'Neill • David Parker • Jim Patty • J.W. (Boots) Rogers • Jessica Polivchuk • Ken Penley • Din Peerani • Shannon Perschon • Al Pettigrew • Milli Pratt • Jody Reid • Eve Renaud • Ron Renaud • Lee Richardson • Larry Ryder • Barb Sartison • Darryl Schmidt • Trudy Selmser • Millie Serkownak • Peter Sharpe • Karen Sklar • Morley Sklar • Paul Squires • ed (small 'e') Stanyk • Andrea Stephen • Patricia Stewart • Eileen Stoffel • Kat Streifel • Phil Streifel • Sheldon Streifel • Barry Styles • Garret Swihart • Rod Sykes • John Tait • Arthur Taylor • Carole Teitelbaum • Glenda Tetreau • Sue Tersmette • Biba Tharp • Bernie Tharp • Lucy Thibault • Don Thomas • Janet Torjan • Alexandra Velosa • Roy Warhurst • Steve Williams • Stacie Woolford • Eddie Wong • Don Wood • Kip Woodward • Shelley Youngblut • Theodore Zurowski